Table of Contents

MW 00880337

A Brief Look at the Characters

Meet Tessa, our Shepherd/Chow mix. Unfortunately, you won't see much of Tessa in these devotions, for she passed away at the beginning of my writing career. Tessa was "my dog" from the moment our eyes met at the animal shelter. Once I picked her up and she laid her head on my shoulder, I knew I couldn't leave without her.

Tessa was a lovable soul who wanted nothing more out of life than to make friends with people and animals alike. She was happy, energetic and loved cold weather. If the weather was cool, we never had to wonder where Tessa was, and sure enough, we would find her in the backyard either snuggled up in her spot by the corner of the house or stretched out in the shade of the cedar tree.

At ten years old, Tessa developed a mass of cancer in her mouth and throat. Eating became painful, and her quality of life began to diminish rapidly. After much prayer, my husband, Jason, and I made the hardest decision of our lives and had her relieved of her suffering. We will never forget her, and she will forever live on in our hearts.

Meet Tippy, our Beagle mix. We adopted her from the pound over ten years ago. I remember looking at her through the cage door and thinking how skinny and malnourished she looked. Her backbone stuck up like the spikes on a dinosaur. Let me assure you that she no longer has that problem.

Tippy is more like a cat than a dog. She loves to eat and sleep. She spends countless hours cleaning herself. She's content to ignore the world when she so chooses, but when she wants to be noticed, she's right there in our faces. Overall, she's very laid back and just goes with the flow. If we're going for a walk, she'll go. If we're staying home, she's fine with that too. The only time she gets really adamant about something is when it concerns food.

Like me, Tippy has had her fair share of health concerns. She had kennel cough and tapeworms when we first got her from the animal shelter. In the past few years, she's developed sensitive skin and arthritis in her back and hips. Additionally, she currently has a tear duct that likes to block occasionally. Nevertheless, she marches on like a trooper. She gives her all and lives her life with true contentment. She loved Tessa dearly but has grown to be equally attached to the newest addition to our family, Mitchell.

Last, but not least, allow me to introduce Mitchell. He's a mess and has been from the moment we rescued him from the shelter. Never in my life had I seen a dog look so lost and alone. A few weeks after Tessa's passing, Jason and I visited the shelter to see if we could find another dog. We knew Tippy needed a friend, and honestly, I had hoped that getting a new pet would help take my mind off my recent loss. I hadn't expected to fall in love, but once I saw Mitch, my heart ached for him. I saw my own pain mirrored in his eyes, and even though Jason insisted that I look at all the dogs available, I had already made up my mind. Mitch was going home with us. . . and he did!

Mitch has no "off" switch. He's all boy and very energetic. In his mind, there's no mountain too high to climb, no river too wide to cross and no squirrel too fast to chase. On the down side, this means he doesn't know his own boundaries, which, you will soon see, has resulted in more than one injury.

Despite his rambunctious nature, Mitch loves to snuggle. He has no idea that 90-lb. dogs are not supposed to be lapdogs. He's lovable beyond belief and very, very protective of his "mommy".

He's nearing six years old, but to the casual passerby, he seems more like a puppy. . . a big puppy, but a puppy nonetheless. With his hilarious antics, there's never a dull moment around our house.

Hide and Seek

A few nights ago, Jason and I were having a simple dinner of hotdogs. I usually try to fix more nutritious meals, but it was one of those days where I needed something quick and easy, and hotdogs fit the bill. Anyway, we were just about finished with our meal when Jason's boss came to the house. We set our food out of reach. Jason went out to speak with his boss, and I decided to use the time to put the rest of the food away.

I noticed right away that the hotdog buns were nowhere in sight. I looked in the pantry, thinking that maybe one of us had already put them away. Nope, they weren't there. That's when I started looking for Mitch. When food disappears around our house, he usually knows something about it. Unsurprisingly, I found him outside pushing dirt over a newly dug hole.

I looked around the yard for the bag that the hotdog buns had been in, but I didn't see it. He usually leaves this kind of evidence. Not finding what I was looking for, I moved closer to his hole. He grew very protective. Now, Mitch is one to bury any kind of bone or treat, but I've never know him to bury a bag, so I dropped the matter, determined to see what revealed itself in the next little bit.

Sure enough, when I went outside a couple of hours later, the empty bag was lying on the ground, and the hole had been dug up. Mitch is a VERY smart dog, so I'm figuring I caught him in the act of snatching the buns, so he decided to bury them until I wasn't looking. That way he could ensure that I wouldn't take them away from him. Smart, but not smart enough.

I'm reminded of the times I try to be smart or sneaky with God. Doing things I know I shouldn't do, oblivious to the fact that God knows exactly what I'm doing. I think I'm being smart, hiding my sin in various holes so that God won't see my rebellion, but I'm not as smart as I think I am. Not only does God see the evidence of my sin (like the empty bun bag), but He sees the entire act.

The strange thing is that I know God is all-knowing and ever-present. I know this, yet sometimes I act as if I don't. I don't know if I simply forget or if I just get so entangled in my sin that I'm oblivious to everything else. Whatever the reason, I'm sure God is sitting on His throne, shaking His head and saying, "Smart, Dana, but not smart enough."

Neither is there any creature that is not manifest in his sight: but all things are naked and opened unto the eyes of him with whom we have to do. - Hebrews 4:13

Help In the Time of Need

Some things are much easier to accomplish without help. Take, for example, my morning exercises. Just like any normal human being, I don't like exercising. I love to hike, but doing a boring workout is just not my idea of fun. However, with my arthritis and bursitis, I have to work at building strength, stamina, and flexibility into muscles that would rather do nothing. So, the workout in itself is difficult enough.

My beloved dog, Mitch, is such a sweet boy. He's always trying to help me. He tries to carry my backpack to the truck when we go for a hike. He's always willing to offer me aid, and that includes during my workout. When I do crunches, he tries to help me up, which defeats the purpose. When I do stretches, he does them with me which has created several toenail-shaped holes in my yoga mat. No matter what the exercise, he tries to find a way to help. I've discovered that if I want to get the full benefits of my workout, I have to lock myself in one of the bedrooms until I'm done. I love Mitch, but his help in that situation is not at all helpful.

I fear, however, that I sometimes treat God the same way. When God steps in to work out a problem, I feel put out if He doesn't help the way I had planned. You see, I've already examined the problem in great detail. I know the best way to work it out. I just needed some time to deal with it. But then God steps in and turns things around completely (and not for the better in my mind). At the time, God's help appears to be only a hindrance.

Many times in a situation like this, I will go to God in prayer. I show Him the plans I had laid out. I explain to Him how I had everything under control. I display the blueprints for Him to see how things were supposed to go. Sometimes, He sets me straight right away, revealing the disaster that was just ahead if I had continued to go my way. Other times, it takes a long while before I realize how, once again, God protected me from myself. He gave me help when I didn't want it and when I felt I didn't need it.

Psalm 46:1 says, *God is our refuge and strength, a very present help in trouble.*

Even when we don't realize we're in trouble, God is already working. Even when we criticize or reject His help, He is there. He offers His help, and whether we realize it at the time or not, it is always helpful (and it doesn't leave holes in my yoga mat)!

It's a Dirty Job

This morning I had the privilege of cleaning dog poop off the bottom of my husband's shoes. Normally, for a task such as that, I would say, "Clean them yourself." (Nice, huh?) But in this case, I know that if he attempted to clean them himself, there would be a much bigger mess for me to clean up. You see, Jason has a serious gag reflex. Certain smells and even sounds can trigger that response, and then it's "Run for your lives!" Unfortunately for me, poop is one of those smells. He just can't handle it. So, whenever he steps in it (which happens quite often in a yard with two dogs), I get to clean it up.

As I stood at the sink this morning, scrubbing away at his black dress shoes, I was pondering how it was I was so lucky as to not be as offended by the smell of poop. Yes, I was thinking of how blessed I was to be able to clean up all the poop, vomit, and anything else that would trigger Jason's gag reflex. Unfortunately, I wasn't feeling lucky or blessed. I was feeling a bit frustrated. After all, I've been fighting a terrible head cold, and the last thing I wanted to be doing this morning was scrubbing poop.

Just as the frustration was beginning to sink in, another thought hit me that completely changed my attitude. Through His still, small voice, the Lord reminded me that I was once covered in something far worse than dog poop. The putrid stench of my sin assaulted the nostrils of a holy God, and I was unable to do anything to remove the filth. That's when Jesus stepped in. With eyes of love and a gentle touch, He scrubbed me clean with His blood and righteousness. He didn't have to. He could have said, "Clean it yourself. It's your sin." But, no! He loved me enough to do what I was unable to do for myself.

And on the heels of that thought, I realized that I love Jason enough to do for him what he cannot. It's a dirty job, but someone has to do it!

But God commendeth his love toward us, in that, while we were yet sinners, Christ died for us. - Romans 5:8

Resting With My Master

I think my dog is ADHD. Mitch is a 90-lb. Shepherd mix, and I'm beginning to think he's mixed with the Energizer bunny. There is just no end to his energy. When he runs through the house, he breaks the sound barrier. He jumps. He dances. He even sings (I didn't say it was pretty). But of all the things Mitch loves to do, three favorites stand out.

First, he loves to eat. It doesn't matter what kind of food or treat it is, the boy can chow down! I think he should have been named Hoover because he vacuums up everything in sight.

Second, he loves to go for a walk. We have to be very careful not to say the word unless we're ready to walk out the door with him because he goes CRAZY. He'll howl and growl until we put the leash on and take him out. He loves to walk, run, and even hike. He's very active and agile, so he really enjoys getting to go off and explore.

Third, he loves to stretch out between Jason's legs and sleep with his head in Jason's lap. Often, at the end of the day, we'll lie in bed and watch re-runs of old shows online. Mitch loves this time because he knows during this time, he gets a lot of his daddy's attention. He rests in Jason's lap while Jason pets him. It doesn't take long for him to fall asleep. It's really sweet (until the snoring begins.)

The other night, we were just getting settled into bed when we noticed a large nose and a pair of eyes at the end of the bed. We acknowledged Mitch and told him he could come up. He jumped on the bed and with an enthusiasm I'd rarely seen walked right up to "his spot" and plopped down, closing his eyes in complete contentment.

The scene made me wonder if I'm that enthusiastic when I rest with my Master. Am I too busy to be content simply resting in His warm embrace? Do I come to him with joy and excitement, eager to spend time with Him? Do I go to Him often enough that I have my own "spot"?

It's something worth pondering. The more I think about it, the more I realize that Mitch and I have a lot in common. I love to eat! I love to walk and hike (although I don't care much for running). And, I too, love to rest in the lap of my Master. I only pray that I can do it with as much enthusiasm as Mitch does.

Come unto me, all ye that labour and are heavy laden, and I will give you rest. - Matthew 11:28

God Works in Mysterious Ways

This morning I went outside for my devotions. I was reading and meditating when out of the corner of my eye, I saw this white blur. I turned to see Mitch running as fast as he could run with his long white rope dangling from his mouth. (Yes, he has his own rope.) He made circles around the yard, running and growling. I can't describe the sight to you, but it was so funny that I laughed uncontrollably. The more he ran around, the harder I laughed. The more I laughed, the more he wanted to run. I guess he liked the approval.

I looked at Tippy, who was just staring at Mitch like he'd lost his mind. "He's a mess. Isn't he?" I said to her. (Yes, I talk to my dogs. Get over it.) But, then the thought hit me of how much we have enjoyed having Mitch as part of our family. He's a real joy. That thought in itself isn't strange, but the thought that followed was. We never would have gotten Mitch if Tessa hadn't passed away.

I believe Tessa's passing was God's way of directing us to another one of His creatures that needed love and care. If you had seen Mitch when he was at the pound, it would have broken your heart. I've seen a lot of "puppy dog eyes," but he was truly pitiful. I've never seen anyone or anything look as lost and abandoned as he did. Today, he doesn't even look like the same dog. He is happy and energetic, lovable and rotten.

He will never take Tessa's place, and I don't think God intended for him to. But I do believe God worked this out, even though it's hard to understand and even sometimes hard to accept. I love Mitch. In just the few months we've had him, he has wiggled his way into my heart, and life with him is VERY interesting. I would love to have my Tessa back, but I see now that the Lord was working things for the good. It is true that God's ways are not our ways. The sooner we accept that, the better off life will be.

For my thoughts are not your thoughts, neither are you ways my ways, saith the LORD. - Isaiah 55:8

I'm Happy That You're Happy

Last week, Jason and I took our two dogs for a hike on a lesser-known trail. Since there was no one there and the trail is not located in a state park, we decided to give them a little freedom. We took off their leashes and allowed them to travel at their own pace.

Mitch, always so full of energy, would run ahead for a little ways and then run back to us. He would run up the sloping sides of the trail, through the woods, then cross to the other side and do the same thing.

Tippy lagged behind at her own pace, stopping every now and then to sniff and mark. Still, she made an effort to keep up, which is more than she'll do when she's on the leash. (She has a bit of a stubborn streak. I think I know someone else like that.)

We walked the trail until we reached the lake, then we decided to see if they would run and play, yet stay within our sight. So, Jason and I sat down on the ground in front of the lake and just spent some time enjoying one another's company. Before long, the dogs had wandered off, exploring every nook and cranny (and mud hole). We spent probably close to thirty minutes just sitting at the lake and allowing the dogs to run free. They loved it!

On our way back up the trail, Mitch decided he wanted to play tag, so he'd run ahead, then circle back and tag one of us when we weren't looking. (Tippy was thrilled at this. NOT!) He ran and played and looked so happy with his wide tongue hanging out of the side of his mouth. I laughed at him until my face literally hurt. Jason turned to me and asked, "What's so funny?" With a huge grin, I said, "I'm just happy to see him so happy."

That thought has stuck with me for several days now. For those of you with children, doesn't it make you happy to see your children happy? For me, my dogs are my children, so I can't help but smile when I know they're enjoying life. Do you think our Heavenly Father is any different? Don't you suppose it makes Him happy to see us happy? I think so. I think He smiles when we smile and laughs when we laugh. I think He's blessed when He sees us enjoying life.

So, what about the hard times? What about those times that life is not so enjoyable? During those times, He knows our pain, and if we can still smile through our tears, He smiles that much more. It's like the song

Rodney Griffin wrote, "God Wants to Hear You Sing." God's happy when we smile during the good times, but He's really pleased when we can still smile through the bad times.

Make God happy today--be happy!

Delight thyself also in the LORD; and he shall give thee the desires of thine heart. - *Psalm 37:4*

Pulled in Every Direction

Jason is trying to get into the routine of jogging with Mitch in the mornings before going to work. However, that dream has not been a reality this week as Jason has been working long days and not getting home until after 9:00 pm.

So, this morning, I decided to take Mitch on a jog/walk myself. Tippy was still settled in bed, so I slipped out with Mitch and walked down the road until I reached the Swamp Rabbit Trail. I took the trail and made a loop back to the house. It was longer than I remembered it being, and I'm not much of a jogger, so we walked at a brisk pace most of the time. Still, it seemed to do the trick as Mitch was huffing and puffing when we arrived home. (We won't discuss my huffing and puffing.)

I was looking forward to sitting down and drinking a nice glass of cold water, but when we arrived at the door, Tippy was there to greet us. Her barks and jumps told me that she now wanted her turn to walk. I obliged her by taking her on a short loop around the neighborhood. At her age, that's really all she needs.

You're probably wondering why I don't just take them both at the same time, right? The answer is simple: they drive me crazy!!!!! They're both used to hiking, and when we hike, they are usually free of leashes and can hike at their own pace. When I try to walk them both on leashes, I feel like they're playing tug-of-war with me. Mitch wants to run ahead. Tippy wants to lag behind and sniff every blade of grass. I just want for both my arms to be pointed in the same direction. Honestly, I sometimes feel like they're going to pull me in two. By the end of a walk, I'm not in a very good mood.

Many times, life feels like a giant tug-of-war. My desires pull me one way while the Holy Spirit leads in another. The world entices me to follow in its footsteps while the Father encourages me to walk by His side. Satan battles me with thoughts of discouragement and defeat while Christ reminds me that He is the Truth. Step after step. Day after day. I feel pulled about like a leaf caught in a heavy current. Twisting this way and that, trying to figure out which way is right. And just like that leaf, I've discovered that it's much easier to just go with the flow. But easier is usually not right.

Just as I split my dogs up for their daily walks, I need to split up the things that pull me in two directions in my life. Unlike my dogs, however, there are certain things that don't need their "turn." I need to limit my daily walks to those with the Father, Son and Spirit. I have no business walking with the others. And if I don't walk with them, they can't pull me around. By focusing on my walk with God, I'll have no choice but to be pulled in the right direction.

How is this accomplished? It's all a matter of focus. Staying focused on God will deter the other things from pulling us around. But don't take my word for it. See what God has to say about it:

Rejoice in the Lord always: and again I say, Rejoice. Let your moderation be known unto all men. The Lord is at hand. Be careful for nothing; but in every thing by prayer and supplication with thanksgiving let your requests be made known unto God. And the peace of God, which passeth all understanding, shall keep your hearts and minds through Christ Jesus. Finally, brethren, whatsoever things are true, whatsoever things are honest, whatsoever things are just, whatsoever things are pure, whatsoever things are lovely, whatsoever things are of good report; if there be any virtue, and if there be any praise, think on these things. Those things, which ye have both learned, and received, and heard, and seen in me, do: and the God of peace shall be with you. - Philippians 4:4-9

If we're truly walking with God, we can't walk with the world, with Satan, or with our own fleshly desires. The Bible says that two can't walk together unless they be agreed. And there's certainly no agreement amongst those groups.

Needing a Nudge?

Mitch is a very smart dog. He picks up on things quicker than most people. Recently, either Jason and I have made the attempt to take him out for a walk or run in the mornings since we're not hiking as much as we once did. The idea was to take him out a couple of times each week, in addition to our hiking days, just to help rid him of some excess energy. Evidently, Mitch didn't get the memo that this was not a daily thing.

Every morning (weekday or weekend, rain or shine) Mitch is up around 7:00, hovering over me and staring at me like a vulture awaiting its next meal. His eyes are bright, and his tail is wagging. He is up and ready to begin his day. My eyes, on the other hand, are heavy, and my tail is far from wagging. The last thing I want to do is crawl out of my comfy bed, walk outside into the humidity and jog two miles. It is difficult, however, to sleep peacefully when a 90-lb dog is nudging you out of the bed.

So, I give up and get up. I pull on my running clothes and shoes, grab the leash and try to sneak out the door before Tippy figures out what we're doing. We walk for a little while, then jog for a little while, then walk for a little while, etc. And somewhere along the way, I realize that I'm enjoying myself. Yes, I'm hot. Yes, I'm tired. Yes, I would rather be in bed. But there's great satisfaction in knowing that I'm starting my day with a healthy habit. There's peace in realizing that I'm doing something good for myself. There's joy in discovering that my weight is coming down and my waistline is shrinking. All of this because Mitch is determined to be my motivator. His nudges get me started in the right direction.

You know, the Holy Spirit is pretty good at giving those nudges too. You know that little tug on your heart that compels you to call a friend out of the blue or send a card to a shut in? That's the Holy Spirit. The strong feeling that you really should or shouldn't go somewhere or do something. That's Him. The voice in your head that says, "You know that's not a good thing. Why don't you do this instead?" That's the Spirit seeking to guide and direct in your life. While His nudges may not be as insistent (or frightening) as Mitch's vulture impression, they are no less important.

When you first heed His direction, you may feel a bit deprived, as I do each morning when I have to leave the comfort of my bed. But within a few minutes, you'll realize how much better things are because you followed the Lord's directions. You'll be happier and healthier. It may not seem like it at first, but you'll never know until you try. The next time you get a nudge from the Holy Spirit, follow His directions and see where it leads. I guarantee, you'll quickly go from feeling deprived to feeling blessed.

*The steps of a good man are ordered by the L*ORD*: and he delighteth in his way. - Psalm 37:23*

It's Our Choice

The other morning I was getting breakfast for my dogs. Mitch wakes up each morning with a growling tummy, so he's very adamant about getting his breakfast. Tippy loves to eat as well, but she has a hard time getting down off the bed by herself. I've discovered that it's easier to fix their breakfast with only one dog dancing around me instead of two, so I leave Tippy on the bed until I have their bowls ready. I set Mitch's bowl on the floor, and while he's eating, I'll get Tippy and then set her bowl on the floor. This usually works well.

On this particular morning, I brought Tippy out, but she immediately left her eating spot and came to me in the kitchen where I was fixing my breakfast. *That's odd*, I thought. Tippy NEVER leaves food behind.

"Go eat your food," I prodded her. No luck. "If you don't hurry, Mitch will eat it." Still she stood there begging for my breakfast. "No," I chided, "this is my breakfast. You go eat your own food." She wouldn't budge.

Finally, I walked her over to her bowl. . . only her bowl wasn't there. It was still sitting on the counter where I had set it to fix their breakfast. I laughed at myself, set the food on the floor, and she immediately started chowing down. (Don't laugh at me. I know you've done something similar. Admit it!)

Unlike Tippy, many times we go hungry and it's no one's fault but our own. I'm not speaking of being physically hungry. I'm talking about spiritual malnutrition. God has prepared a feast for us to sit down to every day. The Word of God. The Bread of Life. It's there for the taking. Whether we eat or not is up to us. God has prepared the meal and placed it in front of us. From there, it's up to us. Eat or don't eat. It's our choice.

But he answered and said, It is written, Man shall not live by bread alone, but by every word that proceedeth out of the mouth of God.
- Matthew 4:4

Trust and Toenails

We have been trying to trim Mitch's toenails for over a week now. When we were hiking regularly, the rocks, asphalt, etc. kept them filed down. Now that we're only going out once a week (sometimes twice), they need some attention.

The problem is that Mitch can't stand for anyone to mess with his feet. In fact, he doesn't like to be constrained in any way. He loves to be cuddled, but if you hold him to where he can't move, he freaks out. We often wonder if he experienced some kind of abuse in his previous home. Anyway, as soon as you grab his feet, he goes wild. He snarls and growls. He wiggles and wriggles. It's impossible to trim or even file his toenails. He just won't cooperate. (However, he does an excellent portrayal of Dr. Jekyll and Mr. Hyde.)

We've tried being firm. No luck. We've tried being sweet and trying to explain why we're doing what we're doing. Still no luck. No matter how hard we try, we can't get him to understand that what we're doing is good for him. It may be uncomfortable for a little while. It may even hurt a little. But in the long run, it's what's best for him.

After another unsuccessful attempt yesterday, I was voicing my frustration to Jason. I was about halfway through my rant when God thumped me on the head and whispered, "Sound like anyone else you know?"

Who? Me?

Yes, me!!!! Just like Mitch, I balk at help that I don't understand. When God is trying to "trim my toenails," it hurts and it's uncomfortable. I don't understand the process, and I can't see the end result. I don't realize that it is, in fact, what's best for me. I fight. I fuss. I whine and complain. I growl and snarl. I wiggle and wriggle. I don't trust my Master.

So what happens? God has to keep trying. The process must be completed. It's necessary. It's in my best interest. How much smoother would it be if I would just cooperate instead of fighting tooth and nail (pardon the pun)?

But as it is written, Eye hath not seen, nor ear heard, neither have entered into the heart of man, the things which God hath prepared for them that love him. - I Corinthians 2:9

On the Right Path

We often take our two dogs out walking at a nearby lake named Lake Wattacoo. It is a secluded place that consists of two or three different trails, a small lake, and a distant waterfall. It's really a beautiful place, and because it is secluded, we find that it's a good place to go to "get away from the world." (Plus, the dogs really enjoy it.)

At one point, there is a fork in the trail that leads out of the woods. Our older dog, Tippy, is precious, but not the brightest crayon in the box, if you know what I mean. She constantly takes the wrong side of the fork, and the bad part is that she doesn't realize she's going the wrong way. I think, in her mind, she sees that we're headed in the same direction and so assumes the trails must lead to the same place. What she doesn't know is that a little farther along her trail, the path turns and basically leads back to where we just came from. So, each time she goes that way, we have to call her and literally convince her that she's going the wrong way and to trust us because we know what's best. Many times, she'll ignore our warnings, only to find herself alone, turned around, and headed in the wrong direction. That's when she starts running back in an attempt to catch up with us.

Just like Tippy, I am sometimes not the brightest crayon in the box. I try to do things my own way in my own strength. My ultimate goal is the glory of the Lord, but I try to accomplish this through my own devices instead of the way He has set up for me to follow. Just like Tippy, I am convinced that since the paths are headed in the same direction, they must end up in the same place. I, too, am often certain that my way is better or easier. And unfortunately, I often ignore the warnings of the Master that I am on the wrong path. Instead, I plod along my trail, allowing the Master to get farther and farther from my view, until I find myself alone and unsure how I came to be back at the place where I started. Oh, if only I would heed the direction of the Master. It would save me from re-walking a lot of trails!

Trust in the LORD with all thine heart; and lean not unto thine own understanding. In all thy ways acknowledge him, and he shall direct thy paths. - Proverbs 3:5-6

Obstacle Course

I don't like walking through our neighborhood because there are so many other dogs. Tippy usually ignores them, but Mitch is far too protective of me to let another dog challenge him. He's sweet, loving and gentle, but if he feels his mommy is being threatened, he turns into Mr. Hyde. Trying to control a 90-pound dog who is determined to "get at" the threat proves very interesting for me at a little over 120 pounds. But no matter which direction we go, there are other dogs to deal with, so usually I take the path of least resistance.

As I tried to take that path this morning, there was a very large dog standing in the middle of the road waiting for us. I don't know if he had escaped from his fence or what, but he was all alone and looked ready to rumble. I turned Mitch around (with great effort) and determined to try Plan B which was to go past the fence with two aggressive dogs that Mitch really didn't like. Still, I thought we could get past quickly and be on our way. When we passed, however, we were greeted by four aggressive dogs instead of two. It took every ounce of strength I had to keep Mitch going forward. He so wanted to protect me.

With this added twist, I decided we would take a different route home. It took some thinking on my part, but I devised a path that should have allowed minimal confrontation. As we took the main road I had in mind, I looked ahead to see two grown cats playing and wrestling in their yard. Just yesterday, I had to battle Mitch because he had seen a gray cat that he wanted to "play with." I knew two cats would be far too great a temptation. That left only two options: go WAY out of the way to get around or go back the way we came. I had a brief, but stern, talk with Mitch, and we hustled our way past the four aggressive dogs. Mitch did splendidly, and I was relieved to finally be through with the drama.

Do you ever have days where it feels like no matter which way you turn, there's an obstacle? You're trying to do what you know is best, but you find yourself staring at one dead end after another. You're trying to serve God, but resistance seems to be your constant companion. If this sounds all too familiar, take heart. There is a way out. Sometimes God will provide a way around the obstacles you're facing. And sometimes, you may have to go through them just as Mitch and I had to go past the aggressive dogs. But do not be afraid, for you are never alone. God will walk with you. He will strengthen you. He will guide you. Trust in Him, and you'll find your way.

Now if you'll excuse me, I need to see if I can get my shoulder back in its socket.

There hath no temptation taken you but such as is common to man: but God is faithful, who will not suffer you to be tempted above that ye are able; but will with the temptation also make a way to escape, that ye may be able to bear it. - I Corinthians 10:13

Unwanted Guests

As I sat on my couch this morning, minding my own business and reading my devotions, I heard the sound of the doggie door. This is not an unusual thing around my house. What made it unusual this morning was that both my dogs were in the living room with me.

I sat quietly trying to hear any sound coming from the back of the house. Nothing. Thinking it must have been the wind rustling the doggie door, I glanced out the window. All was still. Again, I heard the noise. This time my dogs heard it too. I crept through the house and cautiously approached the back door where the doggie door is located. I peered out the window. Nothing. I had just begun to relax when a large black head poked through the doggie door. I screamed. Somehow our neighbor's dog had gotten out of his fenced yard and into our fenced yard.

I used my foot to push the big head back through the doggie door, then allowed Mitch (my 90-lb. shepherd) to help me deal with the "visitor." He chased our guest out of the laundry room and into the back yard. I opened the side gate and shooed him through, then closed the gate behind him. Our guest didn't seem happy to be on that side of the fence, but I know that Mitch is very protective, and I didn't want the other dog to get hurt. He seemed sweet enough, but you never know with dogs.

I had just sat down with my Bible again when I heard the doggie door. This time there was no question about what had come through. The same dog waltzed right into my living room and began exploring my rug. "Oh no you don't!!!" I said as I chased him back through the house. After quite an ordeal to get him out again, I discovered that he had pushed the bottom of our gate open to gain access to our yard. I fixed the gate, and thankfully, I haven't seen the dog since then.

You know, life is full of unwanted guests. Unwanted health issues. Unwanted circumstances. Unwanted thoughts. Unwanted emotions. The key to taking care of these unwanted visitors is to deal with them. We can't ignore them in hopes that they might go away. If I had done that with my visitor this morning, there's no telling how many "surprises" I may have found in my house. Don't ignore them; deal with them.

Once they're dealt with, it's also wise to investigate how they got in to begin with. That way we can work to prevent such unwanted visitors from coming again. Does it always work? No, not always, but it certainly helps. There are things that are beyond our control and that we need to leave in God's hands. However, there are many things we can take care of if we will take the time to deal with them and work to prevent them from coming back. After all, we don't want any "surprises," do we?

Watch and pray, that ye enter not into temptation: the spirit indeed is willing, but the flesh is weak. - Matthew 26:41

Satisfied; Not Satisfied

Mitch is a 90-lb Shepherd mix. He is precious and very-well behaved. But, when Mitch wants something, he WILL let you know. He will howl. He will jump. He will bounce. He will growl. He will dance. He will turn circles. He hasn't done cartwheels yet, but I'm sure it will come soon enough. The point is when Mitch wants something, he won't be quiet until either he gets it or he's reprimanded. (Usually, he gets it. My dogs are spoiled!)

This morning, I was reminded of how adamant he was to get his way. We had planned to take the dogs for a hike up to a local waterfall. As soon as the hiking boots came out, he knew what we had planned. The problem was that he was ready to go right then. We had to finish getting dressed, pack the backpack, take care of a few little things around the house, etc. Mitch doesn't understand this. He understands one thing: GO! (Well, actually two things: Go and eat!)

So, as we were going about getting things ready, Mitch was making his "request" known. He howled, jumped, barked, danced, etc. I'm sure the neighbors thought we were torturing the poor dog. He was hopping around so much that I got tired just watching him. Finally, we were ready to go. We walked out to the truck and opened the door. He immediately hopped into "his seat." We weren't even out of the neighborhood before he was asleep. All that fuss! All that commotion! All that temper tantrum! But, at that point, he had what he wanted, and so he was completely satisfied.

Don't we act the same way sometimes? We want certain things, and we're not satisfied with the things that we already have. Mitch has a nice home. He has a nice bed (unfortunately it is MY bed.) He eats good food. He has a "Mommy" and "Daddy" who love him, spend time with him, and take care of him. All in all, he has a VERY good life. But, it's not enough. He wants more. Aren't we the same way?

We have been so blessed by the Lord, but sometimes we fail to see those blessings because we're looking at the things we don't have. I don't have a big screen TV. I don't have a nice new car. I don't have designer clothing. I don't have this. I don't have that, and I won't be satisfied until I do! When we start itemizing what we do and don't have, our thankfulness will rapidly dwindle, and we'll become unsatisfied with life and what it has to offer us. That leads us to desire more. Then we'll stop at nothing to meet those desires. We'll jump through hoops. We'll throw fits. Hey, we'll even throw away our morals if it will get us the things we desire. More, more, more! We must have more!

The Bible tells us to be content with what we have. Today, instead of dwelling on what we don't have, let's thank God for what we DO have. Our lives will be better, and our souls will be more satisfied. Besides, who wants to hear us howl?

*Let your conversation be without covetousness; and be content with such things as ye have: for he hath said, I will never leave thee, nor forsake thee. - **Hebrews 13:5***

We've Been Warned

On a recent trip to the lake, Tippy discovered a wasp. As it buzzed around her head, she snapped at it. I warned her that she didn't want to do that. Still, even as the wasp flew away from her, she was determined to follow it, to sniff it, to "play" with it. Over and over I warned her to leave it alone. Why? Because I knew something she didn't. I knew that when that wasp got tired of her game, it was going to sting. But when Tippy refused my warnings time and time again, I said, "Fine! Play with the wasp, but you'll regret it."

Sound familiar in your life? I know it does in mine. How often have I disregarded the Lord's warnings and regretted it? Time and again I receive warnings from the Lord. Why? Because He knows what I don't. He can see where my current path will lead me. But instead of heeding His warning, I, like Tippy, decide that I want to do my own thing. Thankfully, Tippy didn't get stung that day; however, I can't say the same about me. I've been "stung" more times than I can count, and all because I didn't heed the warning of the Master.

And though the Lord give you the bread of adversity, and the water of affliction, yet shall not thy teachers be removed into a corner any more, but thine eyes shall see thy teachers: And thine ears shall hear a word behind thee, saying, This is the way, walk ye in it, when ye turn to the right hand, and when ye turn to the left. - Isaiah 30:20-21

Do You Smell Something?

Why do dogs roll around in poop? For the life of me, I just can't figure that out, but I know for a fact that they do. At least, mine do. Not their own poop, mind you, but the poop of another dog or animal. One minute they're walking down the trail minding their own business, the next, their noses are exploring, and before I realize what they're about to do, they push their head to the ground and smear the nasty mess all over. Gross!!!

Unfortunately, dogs are not the only ones who stick their noses where they don't belong. Christians have a bad habit of doing that as well. Gossip. Complaints. Giving "advice" and "suggestions" where they are unwarranted. Yes, we Christians have a knack for sticking our noses where they don't belong and dirtying our lives with the filth of these sins. We often hide our fault under the guise of calling it "sharing a prayer request" or "simply speaking our minds," but the truth is we would be much better off if we minded our own business. I don't know about you, but I have enough of my own faults to deal with to have time to worry about anyone else's.

For we hear that there are some which walk among you disorderly, working not at all, but are busybodies. Now them that are such we command and exhort by our Lord Jesus Christ, that with quietness they work, and eat their own bread. - II Thessalonians 3:11-12

Extra Baggage

Last Saturday we took our dogs over to Chestnut Ridge, a heritage preserve about 20 minutes from our house. The 2.5 mile trail is a moderate, but beautiful hike down to the peace and serenity of a gently flowing stream. It's one of our favorite places to go.

When we arrived at the gate to the heritage preserve, we stopped the truck and got out. The dogs immediately started running to and fro, exploring and looking for a place to go to the bathroom. (We allow them this freedom because they know not to get out of our sight, and they're very well-behaved.)

While Jason and I were getting our gear together, Mitch found an interesting item that he wanted to explore more closely. By the time Jason and I noticed what he had gotten into, it was too late. He had found the skeleton of a rather large animal and decided to roll in it. (Again, I am asking, "why do dogs do that?") As soon as Jason realized what Mitch was doing, he called him to come back to the truck. Mitch stood up and ran over to us but was immediately spooked by something that had hold of his collar. Fear filled his eyes as he ran faster towards us, a large white blur hanging from his collar and bouncing from side to side as he ran. Once we got him stopped, we discovered the item to be the backbone of the skeleton he had rolled in. GROSS!!!! When Mitch had rolled on the ground, part of the backbone had gotten tangled in his collar. Jason had to work it loose and dispose of it. (I certainly wasn't going to touch it!!!)

Mitch didn't know what to think. To him, he was just doing a little exploring, but he got much more than what he had planned on. Not only had he been "grabbed" by a dead animal, but at that point, he smelled like one too. He wasn't pleased. After I had calmed him down, I patted him on the head and said, "That's what happens when you get into stuff that you're not supposed to mess with." WHACK! God thumped me right between the eyes.

Many times in life, we have a knack for getting ourselves into difficult situations. Why? Just like Mitch, we do things we know we're not supposed to do. We go where we shouldn't go, watch what we shouldn't watch, listen to things better left unheard, and say things better left unsaid. We get into things that we have no business messing with and then wonder why things are going wrong in our lives. Just as Mitch got more than he had planned on, so do we when we do the wrong things. Remember the old song, "Sin Will Take You Farther Than You Want to Go"? It's true. We would be much better off if we would stick to the right path and not wander off to go "exploring." After all, who wants to carry around all that extra baggage (especially if it's part of a skeleton)?

Keep thy heart with all diligence; for out of it are the issues of life. - Proverbs 4:23

What Are You Whining About?

I make it a point to always walk Mitch first in the mornings because he is much more adamant about getting out the door. But I'm always amazed at Tippy's behavior while I'm out with Mitch. I can hear her whining before Mitch and I have even left the yard. She whines. She cries. She scratches at the door. She makes pitiful sounds like none you've ever heard. And by the time I get back with Mitch, she's exhausted herself with her tantrum. As soon as I open the door, however, she marches out the door and sticks out her neck for me to attach the leash. She knows what's coming. She knows she's going to get to walk as soon as I'm done with Mitch. So why does she throw such a fit?

As I pondered that thought this morning, I was assaulted by the realization that I act the very same way with my heavenly Father. When things don't go the way I think they should go, I pitch a fit. I whine. I cry. I make pitiful noises. Don't I know that God's going to take care of me? Hasn't He displayed His faithfulness to me over and over again? Like Tippy, instead of anticipating the journey, I work myself into a frenzy about not getting things my way in my timing. Then, when the time for the blessing arrives, I'm too worn out to truly enjoy it. Oh me, oh my!

We have a joke in our family that the word "wait" is the worst of the four-letter words. Mitch doesn't like to wait. Tippy doesn't like to wait. Jason does pretty well in that area, but I could certainly use some improvement. And like Tippy, I need to learn to wait patiently. Her fussing doesn't make me walk Mitch any faster (not that I could go any faster if I tried). Likewise, my fussing doesn't rush God. It simply prompts Him to remind me AGAIN, "Just hold on, child. You'll get your turn."

And therefore will the Lord wait, that he may be gracious unto you, and therefore will he be exalted, that he may have mercy upon you: for the Lord is a God of judgment: blessed are all they that wait for him. - Isaiah 30:18

Who Are You Leaning On?

When I took the dogs for our morning hike today, I decided to take one of my trekking poles on the journey - not for support, mind you, but as a spiderweb catcher. I've discovered that if I wave it in front of me like a sword, I can catch most of the webs with it instead of with my face. To be honest, I felt a bit like Luke Skywalker swinging his light saber. Die, evil webs, die!

When I reached the creek crossing, I decided it would be best to use the pole as it was intended. I was amazed at the speed and ease in which I was able to make the crossing. (I've slipped off the rocks and into that particular creek more times than I can count.) Today, however, my feet stayed dry as I was able to avoid falling due to the support of one skinny, little trekking pole.

I think of the many times in life I try to make my own way. "No, no, God. It's okay. I've got this one." And what happens? Splash! Into the creek I go. "That's not the right path, Lord. I know what I'm doing." The result? Wet socks and wrinkled feet.

Why, oh, why do I constantly feel the need to create my own path or walk in my own strength? I know I can't do it. I know it will lead to a fall. I know I'll be walking around in sloshing shoes for the rest of the day. So why do I continue to do it? I feel like Paul when he said, "For the good that I would I do not: but the evil which I would not, that I do."

My prayer today is that I would walk with the Lord at all times. He alone is my strength, my sword, my shield, and my support. By staying close to Him, not only will I stay dry and safe, but I will also remain on the right path.

The LORD upholdeth all that fall, and raiseth up all those that be bowed down. - Psalm 145:14

My Source of Strength

While at the store yesterday, I purchased a bag of food for my dog. The 20-lb bag was $12.96; the 48-lb bag was $15.96. The choice of which bag to get would have been easy had Jason been with me. However, as I stood there staring at the 48-lb bag, I truly contemplated going with the smaller size. Why? Because 48 pounds is heavy!

My thrifty side refused to settle for the smaller bag, so I gathered my strength and lifted the 48-lb bag off the shelf. That, in itself, was a comical sight, but I wish you could have seen me trying to get that huge bag in the bottom of the buggy. I was down on my knees, pushing from one side and pulling from the other. After much struggle, I had the bag arranged to where it would stay in the cart. The exertion left me weary and ready for a nap. Just as I began pushing my buggy, I noticed that unlike the 20-lb bag, this bag didn't have a pull-off sticker (you know, the kind where you just pull the sticker off and hand it to the cashier). "Too bad!" I declared. "She'll have to figure out a way to scan it herself 'cause I'm not picking it up again."

I continued my shopping. The cashier was able to use a wand to scan the dog food. I pushed the buggy out to my truck, unloaded my groceries, and then stared at the gigantic bag, willing it to hop into the truck on its own. No such luck. With much embarrassment, I finally un-wedged the bag from the shopping cart and dropped it (literally) into the bed of the truck. As I drove home, I deliberated whether or not I could count my shopping trip as my daily exercise.

Indeed, the trip required a great deal of strength. Life is the same way; however, the source of strength should not lie within ourselves. In the grocery store, I had no choice but to pick up the bag myself. In life, I always have a choice. Unfortunately, I usually choose poorly. Instead of trusting in the strength of the Almighty to get me through, I act in my own strength and then fail to understand why things don't work out right.

Weary in well doing? I sometimes think I live in that state, but the truth is that I wouldn't be nearly so weary if I would allow God to lift the heavy loads instead of trying to bear them myself. God is my strength. How many more 48-lb bags do I need to lift before I get that through my head (or better yet, through my heart)?

The LORD is my strength and song, and is become my salvation. - Psalm 118:14

Living In Fear

The month of July has been tough on our family. At the beginning of the month, Mitch was injured rather severely while out hiking. The weeks since then have been filled with expensive vet visits, episodes of bleeding, restless nights and futile attempts to keep a very active dog inactive. It has not been pleasant, but God has been good and helped us through.

As Jason and I were speaking about how to progress once Mitch heals, I made the comment, "I'm scared to take them out by myself anymore. A couple of months ago, he was attacked by a pack of dogs, and now he's slit his paw wide open. Who knows what will happen the next time?" Jason was patient with me (as he always is when I get irrational) and helped me to see that I was living in a state of fear. "You can't be afraid to live life for fear of what might happen," he said. "You just need to live and trust that God will give you the strength to deal with hard times when they come."

I thought about his words. I thought about the two recent scares I'd had with Mitch, but then I remembered the hundreds (not an exaggeration) of pleasant hikes the dogs and I have had. Was I really willing to trade the hundreds of good hikes so that I'd never have to experience a couple of bad ones? Jason was right. I was letting fear make my decisions and rule my thinking. I was allowing fear to keep me from living life. I was dwelling in a land of "but what if this happens?".

II Timothy 1:7 says, *For God has not given us a spirit of fear, but of power and of love and of a sound mind.*

Fear doesn't come from the Lord. So if it's not from Him, where do you think it comes from? It's just another tool Satan uses to get us distracted and off-kilter in our Christian walk. If he can trick us into allowing fear to rule our lives, he's won a great victory. After all, we can't have two masters. God and fear can't both rule. We must choose.

I've decided that once we get the "okay" from the vet, we'll start hiking again with Mitch. We did invest in some dog hiking shoes for him since he's prone to wander off the trail. Beyond that, I am going to try my best to not allow fear to rule my thoughts and actions. Instead, I want to live my life to the fullest each day, trusting that God will see me through any situations that may arise. Life is just so much sweeter that way!

Whiny and Ungrateful

Throughout the past few weeks of dealing with Mitch's injury, one thing has fascinated me: the dog never complains. On the day he sliced his foot open, he licked at the injury, but never whimpered or whined. He only threw a fit when he realized he was without his mommy and daddy at the vet. Since he's been recovering, never a whimper or whine, despite the number of times the wound has been opened and bleeding and the number of times we've had to wrap and unwrap it. He's not thrilled with the process, mind you, but overall, he just hasn't complained. The only sound of discomfort he's made was on the day I brought him home from the vet. He moaned a few times and then vomited up his anesthetic. Those moans were completely understandable.

The sad part is that I've whined and complained far more than he has. I've moaned. I've cried. I've fretted. I've sulked. And I'm not even the one with the injury! Oh, the lessons I could learn from Mitch. Somehow, in his life, he's learned to be strong. No matter what befalls him, he just makes the best of what he has. Why can't I do the same? Why do life's ripples rock my boat so severely? Why can't I be like Mitch, taking life as it comes and doing the best I can with it?

God has been so good to me, yet I find myself unsatisfied with his many blessings. I find myself wanting more out of life. Unfortunately, it often takes one of life's storms (like the one I'm in) to remind me how good my life truly is. As I type this (with one hand since my other is tucked securely beneath Mitch), I long for my "old" life back, the life that I was complaining about just a few weeks ago. It's amazing how much a storm can change our perspective. This one has certainly opened my eyes to how whiny and ungrateful I've been.

I'm reminded of the song, "Sometimes It Takes a Storm." I hate to think that Mitch has had to suffer this terrible injury so that God could point out and correct my attitude, but I must admit that it's a very real possibility. I believe God will do what it takes to get our attention. Not out of spite, mind you, but out of love.

So how's your attitude today? Are you feeling whiny and ungrateful? Does God need to get your attention? I hope not, for I can tell you that the process is not a pleasant one. No matter how bad things may seem, be thankful for what you have. I guarantee you things could be much worse.

For I know the thoughts that I think toward you, saith the Lᴎᴰᵃ, thoughts of peace, and not of evil, to give you an expected end. Then shall ye call upon me, and ye shall go and pray unto me, and I will hearken unto you. And ye shall seek me, and find me, when ye shall search for me with all your heart. - Jeremiah 29:11-13

It's Truly For Your Good

At the time of this writing, Mitch is once again at the vet after having undergone another surgery on his paw. The attempt to remove his stitches resulted in a hemorrhaging blood vessel which had to be repaired. At this point, I have no idea what kind of recovery time we're looking at, and frankly, I'm not sure if my heart can bear to think about it. All I know is that my faith is growing weak, and I'm finding it more difficult to find peace in the midst of the storm.

Nevertheless, I am reminded of a thought that has struck me several times over the past few weeks. Each time we've had to wrap Mitch's paw or administer medication, or place that confounded cone back on his head, I've looked him in the eye and assured him that he was not being punished but that we were doing these things for his own good. Each time I said those words, I felt a nudge in my heart as if God were saying the same to me. "Dana, I know this is hard, but you're not being punished. Believe me when I tell you that this is for your own good. Yes, it hurts. Yes, it's unpleasant. Yes, I know you don't understand. But trust me. I have your best interest at heart."

Before he left for work, Jason looked me in the eye and said, "Spend some time with God today, and find peace." All morning long, I've been asking myself, "How do I find peace? Where do I find peace?" I was struck with the memory of the Sunday School lesson I taught recently. The topic was "sheltered in the promises of God". That is where I can find peace. That is where I can find strength to carry on. Christian author Sheila Walsh says it best: "Jesus is the eternal place of promise, the place where a miracle can happen--because for every problem, there is a promise."

I won't say this is going to be easy because I know better. But I know it is possible, and I'm not alone. God's taking care of me, even if it's in ways I don't understand. The best thing for me to do is to trust in Him and place the entire situation in His hands. He can certainly handle it better than I can!

And we know that all things work together for good to them that love God, to them who are the called according to his purpose. - Romans 8:28

Dog Tired!

Last night was not a good night. It started off fine, but once Jason left for work, it went downhill fast. We had gotten Mitch all settled in for the evening. In fact, he was sleeping quite peacefully on our bed. Normally, once we can get him settled, he stays settled for the night. However, when Jason had to leave at 9:00 last night to go to work, Mitch quickly became unsettled.

For hours, I tried to coax him into going to sleep. I petted him. I talked with him. I hugged him and loved on him. He would settle for a few minutes and then jump up like someone had stuck him with a pin. When Jason arrived home at 12:30 in the morning, I had hopes that Mitch would settle in. He didn't, at least, not until 5:30 this morning.

I honestly don't know what was wrong with him. I took him outside for a bathroom break. I gave him some water. I gave him a little milk. For crying out loud, I even spent some time on the floor so that he wouldn't be cramped in the bed. Finally, at 5:30, Jason and I had had enough. We put him down on the cushion on the floor. Within a few minutes, he was settled. Go figure! Unfortunately, Jason had to get up at 6:30.

As I stumbled around the house this morning, I noticed several things. I was hungry, thirsty and extremely achy. I had visions of chocolate donuts and Pepsi dancing in my head. I even told Jason, "I'd give my right arm this morning for some caffeine." I was joking, of course, but I can't deny that the cravings were definitely there.

As I thought about this, I remembered reading once how when our bodies are tired, they will actually crave other things to try to make up for the lack. My body wasn't really hungry or thirsty (although, I believe it truly was achy). My body was tired, and no matter how many donuts I ate or sodas I drank, my body would still be tired. Why? Because I wasn't giving it what it needed. It needed sleep. Lots and lots of sleep! While food and drink may offer a temporary pick-me-up, they will not fulfill the deeper craving.

I wonder how many times we try to fill our lives with things to fill the void, knowing deep down that only God can fill that emptiness. I'm not just talking about salvation, but even in the Christian walk, it's possible to meet our cravings without truly meeting our need. Our spirit craves time with God, but we're too busy to make that happen. Our spirit craves spiritual bread from the Word, but instead we fill it with television and the Internet. It's no wonder something always seems to be missing. There's a place in our hearts and lives that only God can fill. It's about time we stopped trying to fill it with other things and started giving ourselves what we truly need.

Now, if you'll excuse me, Mitch is napping, and I think I may do the same.

Blessed are they which do hunger and thirst after righteousness: for they shall be filled. - Matthew 5:6

If You Give an Inch. . .

I'm happy to say that Mitch's foot is healing nicely. He's walking and even running some. The muscles are still stiff and tight, but the cut seems to be coming together very well. Our main concern at this point is that some of the stitches are still sticking out. We had thought that they should be dissolved by now, but Jason reasons that since they're on the outside, they have nothing to dissolve into or to aid them in dissolving. This makes sense to me.

Jason's solution to the problem was to allow Mitch to lick at the wound as long as he didn't go at it aggressively. So, we've been leaving the bandages and cone off and allowing him to lick at the area he's been wanting to get at for so long. Most of the time he does very well in being gentle. However, there have been a couple of times I've caught him with his entire foot in his mouth. At that point, I make him stop licking altogether (and, of course, he pouts).

I'm sure that area is itchy. I know he just wants to dig at it, but I also know that would not be good for him (or us). It's just hard to get him to understand the difference between licking and chewing. Licking is fine. Chewing is not. Since he doesn't understand, it is imperative for me to keep a close eye on him during his "lick sessions" to ensure he doesn't go overboard.

I'm reminded of the old saying, "If you give _____ an inch, they'll take a mile." Fill in the blank with whatever is appropriate at the time. For me, it is often "the devil" or "the flesh". Yes, if I give into the devil for just one little thing, I soon find myself far off track, and I don't even realize how I got there. Unfortunately, it's the same with my flesh. If I give in to one little fleshly desire, it undoubtedly leads to another and another and another. It's like the Pringles potato chip slogan: "Once you pop, you can't stop."

Satan says, "One little lie won't hurt," but what I don't realize is how many lies I'll have to tell to cover up the first one. My flesh says, "One more cookie won't hurt," but I fail to take into account how much extra exercise I'll have to do to work off that one cookie. Most of the time, it's easier to just say "NO" to begin with. If Mitch didn't start licking his paw, he wouldn't be prone to chew. If I didn't allow one sin or temptation to trip me up, I wouldn't be so prone to fall prey to the next one.

Are you facing temptation today? Just say, "NO!" Don't give in that inch, and you won't find yourself miles off track (or in Mitch's case, with your foot in your mouth).

Be sober, be vigilant; because your adversary the devil, as a roaring lion, walketh about, seeking whom he may devour. - I Peter 5:8

Wait It Out

Yesterday I had the great privilege of stepping in a nice, juicy pile of dog poop. One of the many joys of owning two dogs, I guess. Anyway, I knew the drill. I scraped off what I could in the grass, limped back into the house, and took my shoes off, leaving them just inside the back door. Why didn't I clean them immediately? Because after so many times of stepping in dog poop, I've learned a few things.

One of the most important things I've learned is that poop is much easier to get off the bottom of your shoe after it has dried. If you try to get squishy poop off the bottom of your shoe, you will only succeed in making a bigger mess (and probably making yourself nauseous from the smell). But if you wait until it's dry, it will usually flake right off, and then you can simply rinse off any remaining residue. Now, aren't you glad I gave you that helpful tip?

Often, in life, we face a similar situation. We find ourselves in a mess, and instead of waiting for direction from the Lord, we try to fix the problem immediately. In so doing, we only succeed in making a bigger mess. Our impatience costs us much more trouble. Many times it's better to just wait it out. Pray about the problem. Turn it over to God. And wait for Him to either fix the problem or direct us to the next step. Either way, it will work out better.

Facing a problem today? Ready to start scraping the poop off your shoe? Be patient. Wait on the Lord. I assure you it will be worth the wait!

Wait on the LORD: be of good courage, and he shall strengthen thine heart: wait, I say, on the LORD. - Psalm 27:14

How Are You Walking?

It's been a couple of days since I last walked my dogs. The first day we forfeited our morning routine, I woke up with some nasty sinus junk, and I could barely sit up, so I figured I could be excused one day. However, the next day I woke up to rain, and I am NOT one of the ultra-dedicated health nuts that will get out and walk or jog in the rain.

So, as I laced up my shoes this morning, Mitch became aware that we were finally going to get to go out again. He literally took off in a run and drug me down the trail. I honestly didn't know my legs could move so fast, but I fear I will greatly regret it in the morning when I can't move. Still, I couldn't fault him for his eagerness. Mitch loves to go. For him, being cooped up in the house for two days is equivalent to twenty years in prison. He had his energy stored up, and he was ready to run.

By the time I got back with him, I was sweaty, sore and struggling to breathe, but I knew Tippy's walk would be much easier. I opened the door to let Mitch in the house while letting Tippy out. I hooked the leash to her collar, and we set out. She didn't seem as eager as usual for her walk. Instead, she seemed eager to sniff. . . EVERYTHING. We'd walk for a minute and then stop and sniff for three. She lumbered along at her own pace, oblivious to anything except her own desires. Finally, I had had enough. I decided I was going to walk, and I would drag her if I had to. I knew I wouldn't have to because after a good scolding, she picked up her pace and limited her stops to a few necessary potty breaks.

I was truly amazed at the difference between their attitudes. One couldn't be stopped, and the other couldn't be made to go. One was thoroughly excited while the other seemed bored. I always knew my dogs had different personalities, but they really proved it this morning.

It made me think of the ways we serve God. Some of us are like Mitch. We can't wait to get out and do whatever it is God called us to do. We're excited and filled with energy. Nothing can deter us from our mission. Some of us are like Tippy. We're content with salvation and long to do nothing more than sniff here and there. We'll check out a few things, and if everything is to our liking, we might comply with a command or two. Otherwise, we're completely focused on our own desires.

It's possible, even, to be like Mitch one day and like Tippy the next. I know I've seen it in my own life. One day I can't wait to serve the Lord. I know what He has laid out for me that day, and I'm excited to get started. Other days, the Lord has to pull me along as I plod at my own pace oblivious to everything but my own desires. As I walked this morning, I asked God to help me be more like Mitch in my desire to serve Him and less like Tippy. Not only will I accomplish more for Christ, but I'll find more joy in the journey. After all, Mitch's walk, while tiring, was uplifting. Tippy's was frustrating.

Are you walking with the Lord this morning? If so, are you walking eagerly beside Him, ready to serve Him throughout your day? Or are you lagging behind, only doing the things that are absolutely necessary? Are you walking willingly or being dragged? Are you Mitch or Tippy?

Serve the Lord with gladness: come before his presence with singing. - Psalm 100:2

Duck Dodging

Okay, it was a typical day with everyday activities. I had just finished my two-mile power walk/jog/flight with Mitch. It was time for my cool-down stroll with Tippy. After all the many days of rain, she seemed a little stiff and sluggish, but nothing unusual. Determined not to wear her out with too much activity at once, I decided to cut down a side street, trimming our walk nearly in half.

We walked along, taking in the scenery and watching for traffic. The sound of yapping alerted us to two small dogs tied up in the yard we were about to pass. Tippy paused, assessing the danger to both me and herself. After being assured that the dogs couldn't get us, she continued her walk, but stopped short when she spotted "it." I had already seen the unusual sight and had turned around to witness Tippy's reaction. Her entire body went rigid. Her ears sloped forward. Her eyes focused on the sight she just couldn't figure out. There, in the yard with the two dogs, was a HUGE white duck. No pool. No cage. Nothing. Just a white duck waddling around the yard.

Unfortunately, Tippy hadn't quite figured things out before the duck spotted her. The duck charged after her. I pulled on the leash, coaxing Tippy to follow me to safety. She'd walk three steps and then turn around to look at the duck. Walk three steps; turn around and look. Walk three steps; turn around and look. Obviously, the duck was gaining on us. I tried to use soothing words with Tippy, assuring her that I was going to take care of her. "Just follow me," I pleaded. "I won't let it get you, but you've got to keep walking." She finally caught on and followed my directions. It wasn't long before we were safely out of Daffy's reach.

Many times in life, we're sidetracked from our journey because we're too busy looking back. Focusing on past mistakes. Second-guessing past decisions. Mourning wasted time or money. And often, waiting for all those things to finally catch up with us. And, like Tippy, instead of trusting the guidance of our Master, we feel the need to keep looking back. Unfortunately, each turn back only leads us closer to danger--the danger of losing our way and getting off track.

It's time we stopped looking back and instead listened to the gentle voice of our Savior as He whispers, "Just follow me. I won't let it get you, but you've got to keep walking." The choice is ours -- follow the Shepherd or dodge the ducks!

Brethren, I count not myself to have apprehended: but this one thing I do, forgetting those things which are behind, and reaching forth unto those things which are before, I press toward the mark for the prize of the high calling of God in Christ Jesus. - Philippians 3:13-14

A Little Dizzy, But Back on Track

Several days ago, on his way home from work, Jason stopped by the pet store to pick up the special food that Tippy needs because of her skin condition. When he arrived home, he entertained me with the story of his wait in line.

The registers are at the front of the store, and slightly behind them are the various rodents for sale. Whoever set the store up was obviously thinking because as customers wait, they can be entertained by the furry critters. Jason certainly was. He told me of two mice who were both trying to use the wheel at the same time. The hilarious part was that they were going in opposite directions. One mouse was larger than the other, so he usually got the wheel going in his direction which caused the smaller one to hold tight as he was flung around and around in the direction opposite to the one he was trying to go. I couldn't help but laugh as Jason was telling me the story. I wish I could have seen it for myself, but he did a wonderful job describing it to me.

Do you ever feel like the little mouse striving for all your worth to get ahead but instead being flung about in the opposite direction? I know I sometimes do. I see the track before me, but sometimes it seems nearly impossible to get to the finish line. I realize that many times it's my own fault. I'm tired or distracted, and I allow these things to cause me to lose track of my goal. Other times, circumstances beyond my control cause my world to tip and spin. By the time I get back on track, I'm so dizzy I can barely stand, let alone walk.

In times like these, isn't it good to know that we aren't walking alone? When I can't stand, I can lean on my Savior. When I can't walk, He carries me in His strong arms. When I can't see the path before me, He leads me. And when my world seems to be spinning out of control, He gives me the grace and strength to begin again.

Sure, it's difficult to stay on the right path when so many things are pulling in the opposite direction. But I've found it much easier when I remember that I never walk alone.

Have not I commanded thee? Be strong and of a good courage; be not afraid, neither be thou dismayed: for the LORD thy God is with thee whithersoever thou goest. - Joshua 1:9

Going in the Wrong Direction

Jason was able to take off a couple of hours yesterday, so we took the dogs up to Falls Creek Falls. It's not a long hike, but it is pretty strenuous. Still, the view of the falls is worth every step.

We hadn't walked far before the dogs began their exploration. Tippy has only recently discovered the joy of following Mitch into "the great unknown." She usually can't keep up, but she's been doing very well lately, so she's been joining him in his little forays into the forest. The problem with Tippy is that she still can't really keep up. She follows him into the woods just far enough to where she can't see us anymore. From there, she's lost because Mitch has already disappeared. What can I say? She has my sense of direction . . . or lack thereof.

Yesterday, they both took off into the woods. Mitch came down to the trail only moments later. Tippy, however, could be heard but not seen, so we called to her. Evidently, she heard our calls, but she couldn't figure out where we were. The next thing we knew, she popped out of the woods and started running . . . in the opposite direction, back toward the beginning of the trail. We called to her, but she only ran that much faster. (In her defense, sounds can really be distorted in the woods.)

We stopped calling to her figuring that if we didn't she'd probably be back at the truck looking for us. We waited a couple of minutes, and when she didn't come back, Jason went to find her. She had gotten a good ways down the trail, covering ground that we had covered only moments before. When Jason caught up to her, she finally realized her mistake, turned around and ran to him. She was tuckered and a little scared, but otherwise unharmed. She made a point of not wandering off the rest of the trip. Poor thing!

I often hear voices calling to me, and like Tippy, I sometimes struggle to figure out from where (or whom) the voices are coming. Is the Lord speaking to me? Are my own desires calling my name? Is Satan luring me away from the tasks I'm supposed to be doing? Whose voice am I hearing? Where is it coming from? At times, it's truly difficult, and I find myself running in the wrong direction, recovering steps that I've already walked or heading off in a direction I have no business going.

I think, it was for these times that God says, "Be still." You see if Tippy, when she first heard us calling, had stopped and listened, she may have been able to figure out which direction to go. But because she was in such a hurry to get to us, she found herself much farther away. In times of confusion, when I don't know whose voice I'm hearing or from whence it is coming, the best thing I can do is to be still. Silence the voices. Ignore the confusion. Resist the impulse to run. Just be still. In that stillness, God will make all things clear.

It's hard enough to climb the hills once. Let's avoid having to climb them a second time. What do you say?

Be still and know that I am God. - Psalm 46:10

Would You Please Hurry Up?

My poor puppies really needed to get out this morning. Because of varying circumstances last week, I was only able to take them on two short walks. Needless to say, by this morning, they had a lot of stored-up energy. So, despite the heat, I decided to take them on a longer hike.

On the way down the mountain, both dogs were full of energy and excitement. They ran and played. They explored. By the time we reached the bottom, however, they were both hot and panting like crazy. I took them the short distance to the lake where I gave them plenty of time to play in the water and cool off. By the time we started back toward the mountain climb, Mitch was refreshed and back into his exploratory mood. Tippy, however, was losing steam FAST!

That's fine. I understand. It was getting warmer, and frankly, I was losing steam too. What frustrated me is that she insisted on walking in front of me at an extremely slow pace. Every time I would try to get around her, she'd speed up. But as soon as I was back behind her she'd slow down again. She was walking so slow that I couldn't even take a full step. I was making little baby steps which was really annoying and tiring.

Finally, I had had enough. Determined to pass her, I sped up to a near jog and cut in front of her. I kept up my quickened pace to make sure she didn't try to cut back in front of me. What I didn't take into account, however, was that we had just reached the toughest part of the climb. For the next little while it was nothing but climbing. Gradually, my pace slowed and slowed and slowed a little more. Then as my legs and lungs felt as if they were on fire, I stopped, bent over at the waist with my hands on my knees, and struggled to take in great gulps of air.

As I stood there trying to regain my strength, Tippy ambled past me. Her pace was slow but steady. She didn't stop when she reached me. She simply continued her climb up the mountain. The whole thing reminded me of the story of the tortoise and the hare. Because of my speed, I needed to stop and take a rest. Meanwhile, Tippy's persistence and determination allowed her to reach the top of the mountain.

Speed and strength don't always win the race. Sometimes all we need is persistence. No matter what you may be facing, don't quit. Keep on keeping on even if your pace seems slow. It's not about speed. It's about determination.

Wherefore seeing we also are compassed about with so great a cloud of witnesses, let us lay aside every weight, and the sin which doth so easily beset us, and let us run with patience the race that is set before us. - Hebrews 12:1

Is That You Final Answer?

Yesterday, I had some errands to run in the morning, so I wasn't able to walk the dogs until after lunch. I grabbed the leash, headed out the door with Mitch and was almost to the road when I heard the most pitiful sound in the world.

What is that? I wondered as I stopped to figure out where the sound was coming from. It didn't take long for me to figure out that the cries were coming from my house. I don't know what was up, but Tippy was pitching a royal fit. Not an angry fit, but she sounded like she was dying. It was the most heart-wrenching sound I've ever heard in my life. I debated what to do, and after one more pitiful howl, I turned Mitch around, went back in the house and grabbed the second leash.

Unsurprisingly, the short walk was unpleasant for all of us. The pace was too slow for Mitch, too fast for Tippy, and my arms now resemble Gumby's because of being pulled first this way then that. By the time we got back home, I was frustrated and wondering why I didn't just ignore Tippy. I knew she was okay. I knew she wasn't hurt. And furthermore, I knew each of us would have had a much more enjoyable and profitable walk if I had not given in to her wailing.

Aren't you glad that God loves us enough that He doesn't always give us what we want? Aren't you thankful that He watches out for us enough that He doesn't give in to our whines and cries. "But God, I want this." To which He replies, "No you don't, child. You just think you do. But if you knew where that would lead, you wouldn't ask for it. I do know where it will lead, and that's why I won't let you have it."

One of the things that made me turn back and get Tippy was the myriad of thoughts running through my head. What if she doesn't understand that this is for her best? What if she thinks I'm leaving her behind? What if she thinks we're not coming back? What if she thinks I don't love her because I'm not taking her first? It sounds silly, I know, but I've had those thoughts toward God, only in reverse. At times, when God wouldn't answer a prayer in the way I wanted Him to, I felt angry and unloved. I didn't understand that it was for my best. I only thought He had forsaken me or was ignoring my cries. Once the "crisis" was over, and I was seeing things clearly, I realized the stupidity of my thoughts. But in the midst of what seems like unanswered prayers, it's easy to be overwhelmed by doubts and despair.

Yesterday, I did not act in Tippy's best interest by giving in to her cries. Not only did I ruin her walk, but I ruined it for Mitch and myself as well. Besides that, I've set the standard: you whine, I come running. And that is not going to work! She will just have to trust that I know what's best for her. As for me, I must remember that a loving "parent" doesn't give in because of protests and complaints. No, a loving "parent" holds firm, even when the child is accusatory and angry, because the parent loves the child and wants what's best for him or her. Just as my heavenly Father does for me.

Thank you, Lord, for loving me enough to not give me everything I think I want!

Hear the voice of my supplications, when I cry unto thee, when I lift up my hands toward thy holy oracle. - Psalm 28:2

Never Satisfied

Sunday evening, we came home from church to find our pantry had been ransacked. Spices lay on the floor. Boxes and pouches sat askew on their assigned shelves. Cans lay on their sides, overturned at some point during the process. And from the way Mitch, turned and ran the other way, I had a pretty good idea who the culprit was.

The thing I have yet to figure out is why. Unlike most Sunday afternoons, Jason and I had been able to come home for the afternoon. That being the case, I was able to feed the dogs right before we left for evening service. So Mitch wasn't hungry. We had taken him for a nice hike on both Thursday and Saturday, so he wasn't overwhelmed with excess energy.

He has never gotten into the pantry before. Never! He's taken a few things off the counter or nightstand when we've been foolish (or forgetful) enough to leave it out. In fact, he once ate an entire pan of banana nut muffins when I left them easily within his reach. But he's never taken anything from the pantry. So, I can't figure out what possessed him to scrounge around in the pantry, settling for the hamburger buns on the third shelf up (nearly six feet off the ground). He bypassed the Pop tarts, the crackers, the open bag of chocolate chips that sat innocently on the bottom shelf. Instead, he went for the buns. How do I know? Because I found the wrapper out in the backyard, along with a tattered bag of instant mashed potatoes. Mmm, what a meal!

The only thing I can figure is that Mitch, like myself, had a battle with discontentment and lost. He wasn't hungry. His needs had been met. But he still wanted more. He simply was not satisfied with what he had. After I got done lecturing him, I had to lecture myself because I act the same way sometimes. God has met all my needs. I've never been truly hungry. I've never been without a roof over my head. I've always had clothes and shoes to wear. In addition to that, I have luxuries that most of the world can only dream of--a television, a radio, computers, a vehicle, a cell phone, and so on. Yet at times, I still find myself wallowing in self-pity for all the things I don't have. I find myself wanting more. My, my, my! How ungrateful I can be!

Benjamin Franklin put it this way: "Contentment makes poor men rich; discontent makes rich men poor." Well said. We are rich in so many things, but without contentment, we might as well not have them. Be wary. Discontentment is one of Satan's favorite tools. It can rob us of our gratitude and shift our focus. It can burden us with discouragement and convince us that God has not been good to us. It can plant a seed of bitterness that flourishes with every area in which we feel we've been treated unjustly. It is a powerful tool that often slips in unnoticed until it has overtaken the mind.

Let's stop ransacking the pantry of life and start being satisfied with the many things God has given us. We have been so blessed. It's about time we started acting like it.

Not that I speak in respect of want: for I have learned, in whatsoever state I am, therewith to be content. - Philippians 4:11

Stillness and Smiles

Each year in November, Jason's parents (who are photographers) gather the immediate family together for a group photo to be placed on the year's Christmas card. By immediate family, I mean Ed and Tina (my in-laws), Brad (Jason's brother), Pearl (their dog), Jason and I, and both are dogs. The entire ordeal is comical and frustrating all at the same time. It is nearly an impossible feat to get all five people and three dogs looking at the camera at the same time, and getting everyone to smile is like trying to cut an oak tree down with a butter knife.

This year, because the weather has been so pleasant and the foliage so divine, it was decided we should do pictures outside. From the moment I heard the plan, I knew we were in for a LONG day. For my dogs, outside time means hiking, especially since we went to a state park for the pictures. We went for a car ride and attached leashes. In the minds of my furry children, they were going hiking, and they were excited about it. The last thing they wanted to do was to sit still for the camera. . . especially Mitch (aka the Energizer Bunny).

It took every bit of effort and patience I possessed to get that dog to be still long enough to take a picture. He ran, hopped, flopped, jumped. He wanted to lay on his back and get his belly rubbed. He wanted to face his mommy and daddy instead of the camera. He was confused and agitated. He didn't want to be still; he wanted to hike! He wanted to commence with his plans for the day, and those plans did not involve staring into a funny-looking black box and being blinded by its bright flash.

Oh, how much I understand what Mitch was feeling, for like him, I do not like to be still. I don't like for someone or something to waylay my plans. I don't appreciate feeling confused and agitated when things are not going as I had foreseen. My natural tendency, just like Mitch, is to try to go about my plans anyway. I'll run, hop, flop and jump, struggling to have my own way, heedless to the Master's pleas to be still.

In my eagerness to do what I want to do, I forget that God has brought me to this place for a reason. We took the dogs to the park so that we could capture their likeness in a picture we could share with others. God has brought me to this place for the same reason, only He doesn't want to capture my likeness, but His own likeness within me. He wants to instill that likeness within me so that I can share it with others. But for that to be done, sometimes I just have to be still. Even when I don't understand. Even when I'm frustrated. Even when I think I know a better way.

You see, what Mitch didn't know was that I had stowed the backpack in the back of the truck early the morning of the pictures. Jason and I had every intention of taking the dogs for a hike once the photo session was done. The reward had been planned and was only a moment away. How much sooner could we have begun the hike had Mitch been more cooperative in the first place? How much sooner could he have gained his reward? How much sooner can I gain mine if I'll only learn to be still?

Lord, I ask You today to show me Your will, but above all else, please help me to be still.

Stand in awe, and sin not: commune with your own heart upon your bed, and be still. Selah. - Psalm 4:4

Through or Around?

On Saturday, Jason, the dogs, and I hiked to the top of Little Pinnacle Mountain. I have news for you: Little Pinnacle Mountain is NOT so little. Wow, it was a tough climb, but the views (especially with the fall foliage) were well worth it. It was a gorgeous day, and the colors were simply indescribable!

As we began, we knew that Mitch would have no trouble with the hike. In fact, we were pretty sure he would leave us in his dust (which is precisely what happened). We were, however, a little concerned about Tippy making the trek. After all, she has some arthritis in her back legs. But we decided to give it a try, and determined if it looked like she was struggling, we would just turn back.

She did surprisingly well. She was tired and couldn't even come close to keeping up with Mitch (who could?), but she seemed to have something to prove. She was determined to do the hike and to do it with as little help as possible.

There were several places where she just had to have help (me too). There were steps that were waist high on me, so obviously, these were beyond her ability. Jason would give her a boost, and she would continue on her way. The funny thing was watching her try to work her way around some of the obstacles. She would go so far off to get around something that she would be completely off the trail and usually headed in the wrong direction. Eventually, we'd have to get her back on the trail and help her around the initial obstacle. So while she thought she was finding a better way around, she was actually just making more work for herself.

After several times of this, Jason laughed and commented, "She would never be able to stay on a trail if she were by herself. She goes so far off track to avoid the obstacles that she ends up going the wrong direction. She'd find herself lost within a matter of minutes."

His comment hit home with me. How often do I do the same thing? Instead of allowing God to help me through or over the obstacles of life, I seek my own way around them. As a result, I find myself lost, confused, and heading in the wrong direction. The really bad part is that, like Tippy, I'm just making extra work for myself because in the end, I have to face the obstacle again. I didn't avoid it. I just prolonged my agony.

There are some obstacles in life that we just can't avoid, so we have two options. We can allow God to strengthen us and "give us a boost" to overcome those obstacles, or we can wander around in the darkness searching for a way around the obstacle. By the midpoint of the hike, Tippy had figured out which way was better. When will we?

Lead me, O Lᴏʀᴅ, in thy righteousness because of mine enemies; make thy way straight before my face. - Psalm 5:8

Shelter in the Shadow

With the weather gradually turning cooler, I'm trying to take advantage of every opportunity to work outdoors. I love to sit outside in the sun. I can write or read. Somehow, I seem to focus better when I'm surrounded by nature. Mitch also loves the chance to run and play. He digs holes, chases squirrels and races with the neighbor's dog along the fence line. Tippy, on the other hand, is not terribly fond of the back yard. Take her on a hike, she's happy. Let her swim in the lake, she's content. But send her to the back yard, and she acts as if I've sentenced her to some form of cruel and unusual punishment. She reminds me of the giraffe on Madagascar, "Nature! It's all over me! Get it off!!!"

So when we're outside, I always know where to find her. She is generally tucked securely behind my chair, resting in the shadow I cast. While there, she is content enough to rest, and she seems more or less undisturbed by her surroundings.

As I watched her the other day, I was reminded of my need and desire to stay in my Master's shadow. I long to find that peace and contentment that can only be found under the shadow of His wings. I seek to be less disturbed by the world around me, and I know that is only possible if I abide in the shadow of the Almighty.

Sometimes, I feel just like Tippy. "The world! It's all over me. Get it off!!!!" And so, just as she does, I seek shelter in the shadow. I guess my fat, little beagle is smarter than I give her credit for.

He that dwelleth in the secret place of the most High shall abide under the shadow of the Almighty. I will say of the LORD, He is my refuge and my fortress: my God; in him will I trust.- Psalm 91:1-2

Fighting for Spiritual Food

My parents were out of town last week, so their dog spent the time with us. Let me tell you, three dogs in one small house is quite a crowd. Cocoa is usually very whiny when he spends time with us. He likes us, but he misses his house and his "daddy", plus I think he knows that Mitch doesn't like him very much. You have to understand Mitch. He's a sweet and precious dog, but he's also very protective, especially of me. He doesn't like another dog coming in and messing with his "mommy."

Tippy is very easy-going. She'll do whatever. She doesn't care who's there and who isn't there. As long as she has her food, she's happy. All in all, I was proud of all the dogs this past week. Cocoa didn't whine, and Mitch didn't fuss. . .until the last day.

I was trying to fix dinner for all three dogs. I had their bowls on the table, and I was dishing out food for each. I went to the kitchen to get something, and the war broke out. Cocoa had sniffed at the wrong bowl. He had the nerve to put his nose close to Mitch's bowl. That was the only excuse Mitch needed to "set Cocoa straight." (What can I say? My dog is a bully!)

My attempts to break up the fight were not working, so Jason stepped in and grabbed Mitch by the tail. Cocoa ran in the opposite direction. (Smart dog!) Mitch was given a firm reprimand for being so grouchy, and Cocoa's minor wounds were tended to.

As I explained to Jason what had happened, I was reminded of the attacks of Satan. He doesn't want us to get our food either—spiritual food, that is. Have you ever noticed as soon as you sit down to a spiritual meal (in the form of prayer, Bible reading, or worship time) he attacks? The phone rings. The oven timer goes off. The drier buzzes. Our minds wander. Our eyes grow heavy. Just as Mitch attacked Cocoa for going near his food, so will Satan attack as we near our spiritual food. The question is how will we respond to his attack. Will we do like Cocoa and run the other way, or will we stay and fight? Just some food for thought today. (Pardon the pun!)

Watch ye, stand fast in the faith, quit you like men, be strong. - I Corinthians 16:13

The Path Unseen

Despite the rainy weather last Friday, Jason and I took the dogs on their favorite hiking trail. Mitch, as usual, was running up and down the sides of the mountain with the vitality of the Energizer bunny. Tippy started off at her leisurely pace, stopping every other step to smell something. But after her warm-up, she evidently decided she was ready to keep up with her brother.

I don't mind Mitch exploring because he has a better sense of direction than I do. He can travel for miles in the woods (off the trail, of course) and still meet us further up the trail. Tippy, on the other hand, has my sense of direction. She couldn't find her way out of a paper bag. If Mitch knows she's following him, he'll usually try to make sure he leads her back out, but sometimes the "explorer" in him forgets to watch out for his sister.

On Friday, it seemed like Tippy knew that Mitch was full of excessive energy, so even though she wandered up and down in the woods, she never let us out of her sight. She was determined not to get lost. The funny thing was how she would come out of the woods. To get out of the woods, one has to go down a slope to get back on the trail. There are places where these slopes are very steep and other places where they aren't bad at all. Tippy would decide that she was ready to be out of the woods and go in search for a way down to the trail. Inevitably, she would walk back and forth along the edge of the slope and then pick the steepest part to come down. Thankfully, she's not too proud to slide down on her behind!

The part that makes it funny is that if she had just kept walking in either direction, she would have come to an easy slope to descend. She stopped too soon because she couldn't see the path ahead. Sound familiar?

Oh, how many times do we feel like giving up on life because we can't see the path ahead? Steep slopes surround us, and we panic. In our despair, we usually choose one of two actions: 1) We try to descend the steepest part of the slope and end up bruised and battered; 2) We sit down at the top of the slope and refuse to go any further. If only we would consider option number three-- Keep going!!!!

God has assured us that He will be our Guide. No, we may not see a way out. Yes, the slopes may look steep. But God is good. He sees what we can't see. He knows what we don't know. He is guiding our paths, and we would be wise to follow His guidance (especially when it contradicts our "common sense"). After all, when we try to go our own way, we may find that we're spending far too much time on our bottoms to get anywhere!

Trust in the LORD with all thine heart; and lean not unto thine own understanding. In all thy ways acknowledge him, and he shall direct thy paths. - Proverbs 3:5-6

Dripping With Blessings

When we came home from church last night, our dogs greeted us at the door just as they always do. We gave them some loving, and then headed to the kitchen for a snack. (Does anyone else get REALLY hungry during church?)

As I was looking through the refrigerator, I noticed there was only a small amount of milk in the container. We had a new jug of milk, so I thought the remainder of the first container would be a nice little treat for the dogs. They love milk! I poured a little into each of their bowls, and they drank greedily.

As they were drinking, Jason and I found a snack and began eating as we stood at the kitchen counter. Mitch, having finished his milk, came in and sat in front of Jason. With the most convincing look he could muster, he stared at Jason pitifully. I made some comment about the "poor starving puppy." Jason replied, "Yeah, his act would be much more convincing if he didn't still have milk dripping from his chin." I laughed, but then a hidden message hit me.

I do the same thing. I go to God with my "wish list." I look to Him with my poor-pitiful-me eyes. "I need this. I need that. I lack so many things," I tell Him. Little do I realize that I have blessings dripping from me. I don't NEED anything. I WANT a lot of things, but that's not the same thing. It is so easy to get into the frame of mind that I've been done wrong. Do you ever feel like that?

"They have the job I want. They have money. They have a nice car. They live in a nice house. They have this, and they have that. I don't have any of that stuff, boo hoo!" What a load of nonsense, but I fall for it time and time again. How dare I stand before God demanding more when I have blessings dripping from my chin!

Thankfully, God is a very patient and understanding God. Still, I don't want to be ungrateful for the many ways that He's blessed me. I don't want to ever lose sight of all that He's done for me. I pray that I will never forget, and that I will be ever mindful of the blessings I've received.

Bless the Lord, *O my soul, and forget not all his benefits. - Psalm 103:2*

Watch Where You Step!

Because of Jason's work schedule, we are not able to take the dogs out hiking on a regular basis anymore. As a result, I've noticed a few things. First of all, none of us seem to have the energy that we had back then. Second, we're all putting on weight. Third, our emotions are not as stable. We're more prone to "the blahs." And last but not least, the piles of poop in my yard have multiplied by a factor of ten. It's not the dogs' fault. (Well, it is, but they can't help it. When you gotta go, you gotta go.) I understand that, but I'm just not adjusted to all the new land mines.

I went out to the back of our property to dump some of the ashes from the wood stove. I had to plot a path around the piles. Anyone watching me may have thought I had been into the whiskey, the way I was weaving back and forth. The path was chaotic, but it was better than the alternative. I hate cleaning poop off my shoes!!!! So, I weaved my way out to the back and then weaved my way back to the house. I was successful in avoiding all land mines.

The whole process reminds me of our walk through life. There are many obstacles in our way that we must avoid, but to accomplish this task, we must pay attention. If I had not watched every step, I could have easily landed in a gushy pile of poop. Life is the same. We must be watchful. We must watch each and every step.

Thankfully, the Lord is our Guide; however, that doesn't stop Satan from planting obstacles in our path. It's our job to be paying attention and listening closely for the voice of our Guide as He steers us in the right direction and out of harm's way. It takes a lot of hard work and a great deal of focus, but it will keep our shoes clean and our lives from smelling unsavory.

So as you travel down life's road today, I caution you to watch your step. There are land mines all about, and many of them are far worse than a poop pile. Watch. Listen. Follow. The Lord will get you through!

Continue in prayer, and watch in the same with thanksgiving. - Colossians 4:2

An Excerpt from The Delaware Detectives: A Middle-grade Mystery

"Abby, can I sleep in your room tonight?" Jamie asked from the doorway after Pop-Pop (that's what we call our grandfather) had sent us off to bed.

"Again?" I questioned. "You've slept in my room every night since we got here. What's wrong with your room?"

"It's creepy. That big stuffed owl on the wall keeps looking at me, and I'm not so sure that it's dead. It looks very alive to me. Please, Abby!"

I completely agreed with Jamie about the stuffed owl. That thing was spooky, and his dark shiny eyes seemed to follow me everywhere I went. I was extremely relieved that I did not have to share my room with that terrifying creature, but I could not let my little brother know how I felt. "You know, for an eight-year-old, you sure are a chicken."

Glaring, Jamie responded, "And for a big sister, you're not very nice."

"All right, fine!" I said as I flopped down on my bed. "But this is the last time. Tomorrow you're sleeping in your own room

—creepy owl or not."

Jamie bounced into the room and onto the bed across from mine. While staying at Pop-Pop's house for the summer, Jamie and I were sleeping in the two upstairs bedrooms. Jamie's room consisted of two beds, a night stand between the beds, a dresser, a closet, and a small table. The creepy owl was the only decoration on the walls. My room was connected to his by a simple doorway with no door. It had similar furniture, but thankfully, no stuffed owl. My room also contained the attic doorway, a small cut-out in the wall covered by a plywood door that fastened with a simple latch.

As I turned out the light that night, I wondered how I was going to fulfill my plan. I wanted to look in the attic again, but how was I going to sneak in there with my little brother in the same room? I thought about it for several minutes until I heard the soft, even breathing coming from the other side of the room.

"Jamie, are you awake?" I asked.

No answer.

"Jamie," I said a little louder. "Are you awake?"

Still, no answer. *My plan might just work*

out after all, I thought. I knew my brother to be a heavy sleeper, so I slipped out of my bed and put on my pink robe and fuzzy slippers. I grabbed my "emergency bag" from beside my nightstand. This bag contained a few snacks, a couple of sodas, a book, and some other odds and ends. I never went anywhere without my bag.

I tiptoed across the room to the attic doorway and slowly lifted the latch. As I swung open the small door, it made a terrible scraping sound. I looked back over my shoulder to see if Jamie had awakened. He was lying in the same position with his eyes closed. I breathed a sigh of relief, crept through the doorway, and shut the door behind me. In the darkness, I felt along the walls for a light switch. I knew there had to be one because Pop-Pop had turned the lights on when we were in the attic this morning. I was beginning to lose hope of finding it when I felt something tickling my face. I reached up, and my hand came in contact with something that felt like a long string. I grabbed it, gave it a tug, and the attic lit up.

I blinked at the sudden brightness and then made my way towards the old dusty book I had found earlier that day. When I spotted it, I settled down on the floor and placed it in my lap. As I opened the book and looked through the many pages of stamps, I could not help but be excited. I love old stuff! It felt like Christmas to me.

I first discovered the stamp collection when Jamie and I were exploring the attic this morning. At first glance, it appeared to be an old photo album, but as soon as I opened it, I knew we had found something special. This collection was awesome and probably worth a lot of money. There were even stamps dating back to the 1800s. Being a history lover, I practically drooled as I turned the yellowed pages.

I don't know how long I had been in the attic when I felt a pang of hunger. Thinking how smart I had been to bring my "emergency bag," I grabbed the bag and rummaged through it. "That'll work!" I said to myself, pulling out a bag of chips and a soda. I had only just begun to enjoy my snack when I heard a quiet thump.

Oh, please don't be a rat! I thought. I sat still trying to decide from which direction the sound had come, but the sound had stopped. I was beginning to think I had imagined the noise until I heard it again, and this time I was sure it was something much bigger than a rat.

"AAUUGGHH!" I screamed as I jumped up, dropping my chips, my drink, and the stamp collection. I looked toward the source of the noise but couldn't see past the brightness of the attic light. All I could make out was a dark figure moving towards me from the shadows. I stepped back. The figure came closer until it stood directly under the light. "Jamie? You scared me half to death! What are you doing up here?"

"I woke up a little while ago and thought that you had gone to the bathroom. But when you never came back, I thought maybe you had come back up here. I guess I was right."

"How did you open the door without making any noise? It let out a terrible scrape when I opened it."

"I don't know," Jamie said. "Maybe it just doesn't like you."

"That's the dumbest thing I've ever heard. How can a door like or dislike someone? Go back to bed, Jamie. I'll be there in a few minutes."

I looked down at the book on the floor and groaned. The stamp collection was lying next to a puddle of brown liquid, and at least one page was splattered with soda.

"Look what you did!" I snapped at Jamie.

"Now there's soda all over Pop-Pop's book. We're going to be in big trouble!"

"We? I didn't spill the drink," Jamie said defensively.

I got down on my knees and slid the book away from the sticky mess. "I wouldn't have spilled it either if you hadn't startled me. What am I going to do? Quick, Jamie, go get some towels!"

"I didn't make the mess. You go get the towels!"

"Jamie," I said through gritted teeth, "please just go get something for me to dry this off with."

"Fine," he said, "but I'm not cleaning it up."

In minutes, he returned with a towel. I picked up the soggy chips and the now-empty can of soda and wiped up the spill with the towel. As I picked up the stamp collection to dry it off, several of the stamps fluttered to the floor. "Great," I muttered. "I guess the moisture caused the glue to wear off. Now these things won't stick anymore. I am dead meat!"

"Yep, you're right!" Jamie said.

I glared up at him. "Well, don't just stand there. Help me pick them up."

With a sigh, Jamie bent down and helped me pick up the stamps.

"Hey," I said after a few minutes. "Look at this one. The back of this stamp has the letter 'E' on it. That's strange. I wonder what it means."

Jamie shrugged his shoulders and continued picking up the stamps. Suddenly he stopped and turned to me. "This one has a letter on it too—the letter 'W.'"

Immediately, I began to turn over the stamps that had fallen out of the book. Most of them—but not all—had a single letter written on the back of the stamp. "T, D, H, N, E, U, S, O, E, F, C, E, R, B, E, Y, T, A, M," I said as I looked at the row of letters. "What could they mean?"

Jamie's dark eyes lit up. "Maybe it's a secret message."

"Yeah, right!" I said.

"No," Jamie protested. "I'm serious. Maybe someone gave this to Pop-Pop, and this secret message leads to a treasure or something. That stuff happens all the time."

I looked at my brother.

"Well," he mumbled, "it happens a lot in books and movies."

"You have quite an imagination," I said. "If this was a secret message to Pop-Pop, he would have found it a long time ago. It's probably just some old letters that meant something to someone at some time. I wonder though. . ."

"What?" Jamie asked.

"I just wonder if there is anything on the backs of these other stamps, you know, the ones that didn't get wet."

"Well," Jamie said, glancing at the book and grinning, "there's only one way to find out."

"Are you crazy? I'm already going to be in trouble. You want me to take more of them out of the book? No way!"

"But it's the only way we'll know if anything is on the back of them. Come on! Don't you want to see the backs of them? Don't you want to know?" Jamie said.

I knew better than to listen to him. After all, the letters were probably nothing. But my curiosity beat out my common sense, and I began to carefully remove each stamp. I started with the page that was splattered with drink. Some of the stamps that had not fallen off were damp, which made them easy to remove. I turned over each stamp as I lifted it from the book. Just as with the others, most of them had various letters on the back, but they were jumbled and made no sense. However, as I started on the next page, I found that the letters actually spelled out words. The stamps that were blank on the back were placed in between words as if to separate them. Once Jamie and I had removed and turned over all the stamps on the second page, the message was clear: w*here the water goes round and round.*

"What does that mean?" Jamie asked as he read the message aloud.

"I have no idea, but that's probably not all of the message."

Jamie stood up and stretched his back and legs. "What do you mean?"

I pointed to the stamps that were spread out in front of me. "I mean that we still have all of these letters from the first page. They probably spell out the first part of the message, but I don't know how we're ever going to unscramble them."

"Don't you remember how they were laid out in the book?" Jamie asked. "The letters were probably in order just like they are on this page."

"No, I don't remember," I said with frustration. "I had just started to look at this page when you came up and scared—um—startled me."

I just stared at the letters, but Jamie sat down again and turned the stamps from the second page face up.

"What are you doing?" I asked.

"I'm just looking at something," he answered as he studied the page.

After several minutes, Jamie smiled. "Yep," he said, "that's what I thought."

"What?" I asked, puzzled.

"Look at the stamps on this page real close."

I studied the rows of faces looking back at me—George Washington, Abraham Lincoln, Benjamin Franklin. I studied the color of each stamp, from eerie yellows to rosy reds. "Okay, I don't get it. What am I looking for?"

Jamie gave another sigh. "Do I have to do everything? Look at the dates."

I turned my attention back to the page and gasped in excitement. "They're in chronological order!"

"Chrono-what?" Jamie asked.

"Chronological order. It means in order of the dates. See." I pointed at the first stamp on the page and moved my finger across the page. This first one here was made in 1881, and this next one, 1882, then 1883, and so on. All we have to do is put the stamps in order by the year they were made, and we'll have the first part of the message."

"I know that," Jamie snapped. "I'm the one who told you they were in order. Remember?"

"It doesn't really matter. The important thing is that now we can read the message."

As we sorted through the stamps, I could not believe I had overlooked something so simple. How embarrassing to be outsmarted by my little brother! Luckily, no one else was there to see, but that didn't keep him from smiling that ridiculous *I'm-so-smart* smile.

After several minutes, we had the first page of stamps in order. We turned them over so that we could see the writing on the back of each stamp and stared at the message that was spread before us. "The secret may be found where the water goes round and round," I read aloud.

"Yes!" Jamie shouted. "I knew it. It *is* about a secret treasure! I told you so!"

"We don't know that," I said, but I was beginning to wonder if he might be right. Could this be a clue to a hidden fortune? If so, what in the world did it mean?

Available in paperback
and all e-book formats.
http://www.danarongione.com/
#!the-delaware-detectives

An Excerpt from Random Ramblings of a Raving Redhead

Stop and Smell the Skunk?

On our way to church Sunday morning, we ran over a skunk. We came up over the hill, and there he was lying in the road. We didn't have time to swerve and miss him. Needless to say, it was a VERY long ride to church. We rolled the windows down, hoping that the fresh outside air would help to get rid of some of the smell. We noticed that as long as we were moving, the smell wasn't too bad. If we stopped, however, the fragrance was overwhelming. It stunk so bad that I could taste it. In fact, it was so bad that I was afraid my clothes were going to start smelling skunk-like as well. So we did our best to keep moving. . .that is, until we got to church. (I won't even go into the smell that awaited us when we got out of church that afternoon. Let's just say it wasn't pleasant.)

You know, sometimes life stinks. Things happen that we feel shouldn't. Daily circumstances don't always meet our qualifications for a good day. All in all, it stinks just like the skunk we hit (may he rest in pieces, er, peace). But if we sit around thinking about how bad things are, the smell (or circumstance) won't get any better. In fact, it will get worse. The best way to deal with the smell is to keep moving. Keep going. Keep running the race. Keep serving the Lord. Don't focus on the smell, focus on doing all you can to please the Lord. As we do, the smell starts to wear off to the point that we hardly notice it anymore. Praise the Lord!

(BTW, if you're riding down 183 towards Pickens any time in the near future, watch out for Pepe La Pew! He's hard to miss.)

For God is not unrighteous to forget your work and labour of love, which ye have shewed toward his name, in that ye have ministered to the saints, and do minister. And we desire that every one of you do shew the same diligence to the full assurance of hope unto the end. - Hebrews 6:10-11

The Bird and the Bread

I saw the funniest thing this past Saturday. I was cleaning up the fellowship building at our church after brunch. As I pushed the broom past the window, I stopped. A huge black bird was in the yard. His mouth was full of the toast that we had thrown out. It was really a comical sight--this black bird with a mouth full of white toast. And, his mouth was completely full. The toast was sticking out of each side of his beak. It was hilarious.

The thing that caught my attention next was that he kept trying to pick up more and more of the toast. "Don't be greedy," I heard myself saying. But he didn't listen. He tried in vain over and over again to pick up another piece of toast, but his beak was just too full. Finally, in frustration, he put his mouthful down on the ground and picked up the single piece that was giving him so much trouble. Then he tried to pick up the mouthful again. It didn't work. After several minutes, he flew off with the single piece in his beak, leaving the mouthful on the ground. Stupid bird!

But then I started thinking. We're the same way, aren't we? We go through life always trying to get more. Maybe we're not all striving for more possessions, but how about more time, more energy, or better health? Just like the black bird, our lives are full of blessings, but in frustration, we set them all aside so that we can pick up one more thing. We fool ourselves into thinking we can have it all, but just like the bird, we find that we can't handle all those blessings at one time.

It would do us all good to remember the black bird. Let's not sacrifice all of today's blessings because of greed. Let's take today's blessings and enjoy them. God will send more when we need them. Let us be content with what we have and raise our voices to Heaven as we say, "We have enough!"

And God is able to make all grace abound toward you; that ye, always having all sufficiency in all things, may abound to every good work. (II Cor. 9:8)

The Plant Whisperer

I don't have much of a green thumb. In fact, I can guarantee you that if I receive a plant of any kind, it will be dead within 72 hours. Giving me a plant is like condemning it to death. I once had someone give me a miniature rose bush. She assured me that I could not kill it. "Just put it in the ground where it can get both sun and shade, and it will grow." I followed her instructions. The poor thing didn't stand a chance. It was dead within the week. Plants are not my thing!

One thing I do know about plants is that they require two things: water and sunshine. Without these essential elements, the plant will wither and die. With them, the plant can thrive and grow, often times producing fruit.

The Christian life is the same way, for it, too, requires two things: the Bible and prayer. Without them, the Christian life will wither and die. With them, the Christian can thrive and grow, often times producing fruit. Isn't the similarity astounding?

Another similarity between plants and Christians is that it takes time for "the seed" to grow into what it's meant to be. When you first plant a seed, it may be weeks or even months before you see any evidence of change in that seed. You've watered it. You've given it plenty of sun. But, still, you see no results. (In my case, that's probably because I've already killed it, but for the rest of you, this is a normal stage in the process of growth.) Sometimes the Christian life is that way. We read our Bible and pray, but we still don't see the growth we long for. Just as with the plant, what we don't see is the change that is occurring under the surface.

Are you frustrated today because you don't see the growth in your Christian walk that you would like to see? Are you questioning your usefulness because it seems that you haven't made a difference in this world? Are you despairing of ever seeing fruit for your labors? If so, I beg of you, don't quit taking care of your seed. Nourish it. Water it with the Word. Expose it to the light of God's truth and goodness. And then, when you least expect it, you'll see the beginnings of the growth you've longed for. But be warned. If you forsake the care of your seed, it will wither and die. The choice is yours. Choose wisely!

But grow in grace, and in the knowledge of our Lord and Saviour Jesus Christ. To him be glory both now and for ever. Amen. - *II Peter 3:18*

No Labels Required

On my way home from running errands yesterday, I saw an unusual (and rather comical) sight. An old, beat-up truck was pulled over to the side of the road. A man, tools spread all around him lay on the ground underneath the uncooperative vehicle. That's not the part that's unusual or comical. What was funny was that painted in large yellow letters on the tailgate of the truck was the word "CLUNKER." My first thought was, *No kidding!*

Don't get me wrong. I'm not belittling the fellow for having an old vehicle. Jason's bronco, *The Beast*, is almost as old as I am. It could appropriately be labeled as "CLUNKER," but don't tell Jason I said that. I understand that we have to make do with what we have. I just found it amusing that whoever painted that title on the vehicle felt that it was necessary. Anyone could look at truck and tell it was a clunker. No label was required

The whole thing caused me to think about whether or not I need a label. When people look at me, is it obvious that I'm a Christian? Are my words, my actions, and my attitudes good representations of Christ? Am I living up to what God called me to be?

I've met many people who call themselves Christians, but I would have never made the connection. I can't judge their hearts, for only God knows whether or not they've trusted in Him. But, I can see their attitudes and actions. I can hear their foul language. Their mean-spirited nature is evident. If not for their "Christian label," I would have pegged them for those lost and on their way to Hell.

If we have to tell others that we are Christians, we're evidently not doing a very good job at representing Christ. Just as it was obvious that the old truck was a clunker, so should it be obvious that we are Christians. No labels should be necessary!

Now when they saw the boldness of Peter and John, and perceived that they were unlearned and ignorant men, they marvelled; and they took knowledge of them, that they had been with Jesus. - Acts 4:13

A Boatload of Blessings

And it came to pass, that, as the people pressed upon him to hear the word of God, he stood by the lake of Gennesaret, and saw two ships standing by the lake: but the fishermen were gone out of them, and were washing their nets. And he entered into one of the ships, which was Simon's, and prayed him that he would thrust out a little from the land. And he sat down, and taught the people out of the ship. Now when he had left speaking, he said unto Simon, Launch out into the deep, and let down your nets for a draught. And Simon answering said unto him, Master, we have toiled all the night, and have taken nothing:

nevertheless at thy word I will let down the net. - Luke 5:1-5

I want you to picture this story through your mind's eye. Jesus, standing tall at the edge of a great body of water. People gathered all around him, hanging on his every word. Two empty boats bobbing up and down on the water's surface.

Now, look off to the side. A group of fishermen sit huddled together, scrubbing their nets (not that they needed cleaning-- after all, they had remained empty all night). Take a close look at these men. Their eyes bespeak weariness. Their expressions portray disappointment. Their posture indicates defeat. They had labored all night and had absolutely nothing to show for it. There was no fruit for their labor. There was no evidence that they had been hard at work. There were no fish, which meant there was no money. After all, fishing was their job.

If you listen carefully, you can even hear their conversation. "What do you think went wrong?" asks one fisherman. "I don't know," answers another. "Maybe this isn't what the Lord called us to do after all." "What's the use?" cries a third fisherman. "It's just too hard, and it's not fair. We work just as hard as the other fishermen. Why do they get all the profits while we sit here with empty nets and heavy hearts?"

Have you ever found yourself in a similar situation? Whether it be your job, your family, your church, or something else entirely. You put your effort into it day after day only to be rewarded with pain and disappointment. You work hard, doing the tasks that you believe God has called you to do, and NOTHING! No fruit! No reward! No compensation! Nothing but the bitter taste of defeat. You feel like giving up. You feel like changing directions. You question if maybe you heard God wrong, and this is not His will after all. But most of all, you doubt. You doubt if God even cares about you or what you're going through. Sound familiar? If so, read on

And when they had this done, they inclosed a great multitude of fishes: and their net brake. And they beckoned unto their partners, which

were in the other ship, that they should come and help them. And they came, and filled both the ships, so that they began to sink. When Simon Peter saw it, he fell down at Jesus' knees, saying, Depart from me; for I am a sinful man, O Lord. For he was astonished, and all that were with him at the draught of the fishes which they had taken. - Luke 5:6-9

Did you catch what just happened? The fishermen had toiled all night (the best time for fishing, mind you) and hadn't caught a thing. But, now, in God's time, they caught so many fish that their nets broke and two boats started to sink under the weight. (Imagine the smell!)

God still works miracles today, but He does so in His own time, just as He has always done. His ways are not our ways. They may not make sense to us. They may not seem the best to us. But if we will allow Him to lead us and if we will be faithful to follow that leadership, we will see miracles. Our disappointment will be replaced with great joy. We will be able to trade our defeat for victory. But we must wait on God. It's difficult, I know, but miracles don't happen without Him.

If you're weighed down with questions today about God's purpose for you and your ministry, talk to God about it. Follow His leadership, and then wait for His miracle. It will come, but only in His time! And when it does come, it will take more than two boats to hold the blessings!

*Available in paperback
and all e-book formats.
http://www.danarongione.com/
#!random-ramblings-of-a-raving-redhead*

Products by Dana Rongione

Random Ramblings of a Raving Redhead - Grab a cup of hot chocolate and join me on a journey of personal experience combined with heartfelt encouragement and fun-filled observations. With a giggle here and a sniffle there, you'll uncover new insights to lift your spirit, lighten your load, and comfort your heart.

The Deadly Darts of the Devil - As Christians, we must battle Satan each and every day. It is our duty to be aware of the weapons that he uses so that we may better defend ourselves against his attacks. This book explores ten of the deadly darts used by Satan to weaken our faith and hinder our Christian growth.

There's a Verse for That - Satan is attacking. You need a weapon, and you need it fast! You wrack your brain trying to remember the verses you have hidden in your heart, but your mind draws a blank. You're tired. You're weary. You're confused. You flip through your Bible looking for. . .for what? You don't even know. What you do know is that you need to hear from God soon or you'll lose this battle. Never fear. The answer is now at your fingertips. Whether you're lonely or afraid, discouraged or sad, **There's a Verse For That** can lead you to the scripture you need to find peace, direction, and encouragement. **There's a Verse For That** is not a substitute for the Bible. It is a map that will lead you to a very present help in the time of need.

The Delaware Detectives - What do the following have in common: a muntjac deer, a toilet, and a hairless cat? They are three key factors in uncovering a treasure that may or may not exist. But for Abby and Jamie Patterson, these items are essential ingredients to fulfilling their grandfather's greatest desire. Is the fortune real, or are the siblings following a path to nowhere as set down by an eccentric old woman? The quest is on, and time is running out.

God Can Use My Differences - Vicki shivered and walked through the doors of the hospital. She didn't want to be there, but the doctors said they could fix her face. And oh, how she wanted them to fix it! Since birth, Vicki suffered from a condition called a cleft palate. This happens when parts of the face don't form correctly. Because of this, Vicki looked different than most children. A few children pointed and laughed when they saw Vicki, but most screamed or cried. Vicki knew why. She thought she looked like a monster and felt sorry for herself because she didn't have any friends -- that is, until she met Mandy, a little girl born with a disability of her own.

Improve Your Health Naturally - Are you ready to lose weight and improve your health? Are you tired of taking prescription drugs? Is pain keeping you from doing all the things you once enjoyed? With just a few small changes to your daily routine, you can finally get on the road to recovery. Set yourself free from the pain of arthritis, the agony of migraines and the irritation of acid reflux. Regain your energy and vigor for life. Reduce stress, and find peace. Do it all naturally!

A Word Fitly Spoken – Daily devotions by Dana Rongione, weekly Christian comedy, and the occasional Christian book review. Subscribe via Kindle or sign up to receive the daily newsletter. http://DanaRongione.blogspot.com

Song of the Day – Begin each day with a dose of Southern Gospel and Contemporary Christian music. http://ChristianSongoftheDay.blogspot.com

Regular Podcasts - Dana records her weekly Sunday School lessons and other speaking engagements. These audio tracks/podcasts are available at no charge for your listening pleasure. http://sermon.net/wordfitlyspoken

Facebook Page –

http://facebook.com/danarongione.author

DanaRongione.com – The website of Christian author and speaker, Dana Rongione. Browse through her articles, read her blogs, purchase her products, book her for a speaking engagement, contact her, and much more.
http://DanaRongione.com

14289765R00076

Made in the USA
Charleston, SC
02 September 2012